THE SPIRITUAL LIFE

THE SPIRITUAL LIFE
THE TEACHING OF THOMAS GOODWIN

AS RECEIVED AND REISSUED

BY

ALEXANDER WHYTE, D.D., LL.D.

AUTHOR OF
'BIBLE CHARACTERS' 'BUNYAN CHARACTERS'
'LANCELOT ANDREWES' 'JACOB BEHMEN' 'SANTA TERESA'
'SIR THOMAS BROWNE' 'RUTHERFORD'S CORRESPONDENTS'
'FATHER JOHN' ETC.

VOL. I.

WIPF & STOCK · Eugene, Oregon

Wipf and Stock Publishers
199 W 8th Ave, Suite 3
Eugene, OR 97401

The Spiritual Life
The Teaching of Thomas Goodwin, As Received
and Reissued by Alexander Whyte
By Whyte, Alexander
ISBN 13: 978-1-4982-9496-6
Publication date 5/28/2016
Previously published by Oliphants, 1900

TO
JOHN KELMAN

I had hoped this would have been my least imperfect work: but, being what it is, its publication seems to carry with it some sort of irreverence toward the great saint in whose name I began to write years ago, and with whom I end. But I have done my best, bearing in mind that I have no right to reckon on the future.—

NEWMAN'S *Advertisement to his "Athanasius."*

TABLET IN PORCH OF CITY TEMPLE LONDON

THE CHURCH ASSEMBLING HERE
WAS FOUNDED IN SIXTEEN HUNDRED AND FORTY,
BY THE

REV^D THOMAS GOODWIN, D.D.,

PREACHER TO THE COUNCIL OF STATE,
PRESIDENT OF MAGDALEN COLLEGE, OXFORD,
MEMBER OF THE WESTMINSTER ASSEMBLY OF DIVINES,
CHAPLAIN TO OLIVER CROMWELL.

THE CHURCH FIRST MET IN ANCHOR LANE, THAMES STREET;
THENCE REMOVED IN 1672, TO PAVED ALLEY, LIME STREET;
THENCE IN 1755, TO MILES LANE;
THENCE IN 1776, TO CAMOMILE STREET;
FROM
THENCE IN 1819, UNDER THE MINISTRY OF THE
REV^D JOHN CLAYTON,
TO THE POULTRY, CHEAPSIDE;
AND THENCE IN 1873, UNDER THE MINISTRY OF
JOSEPH PARKER, D.D.,
TO THE SOUTH-WESTERN END OF HOLBORN VIADUCT.

THIS TABLET
IS ERECTED BY THE CHURCH TO PERPETUATE
THE HALLOWED MEMORY OF
HER VENERABLE AND ILLUSTRIOUS
FOUNDER.

EPITAPH COMPOSED BY THOMAS GILBERT, B.D., FOR INSCRIPTION ON TOMB IN BUNHILL FIELDS, LONDON

THOMAS GOODWIN, S. T. P.,
AGRO NORFOLCIENSI ORIUNDUS;
RE ANTIQUARIA, PRÆSERTIM ECCLESIASTICA,
NEC ANGUSTÆ LECTIONIS, NEQUE INEXPEDITÆ.
SACRIS SI QUIS ALIUS SCRIPTURIS PRÆPOTENS,
INVENTIONE ADMODUM FERACI,
NEC SOLIDO MINUS SUBACTOQUE JUDICIO,
VARIIS INTER SE LOCIS ACCURATE COLLATIS
RECONDITOS SPIRITUS SANCTI SENSUS
MIRA CUM FELICITATE ELICUIT.
MYSTERIA EVANGELII NEMO MORTALIUM
AUT PERITIUS ILLO INTROSPEXIT
AUT ALIIS CLARIUS EXPOSUIT.
MATERIAM, FORMAM, REGIMEN, OMNIA,
ECCLESIARUM A CHRISTO INSTITUTARUM,
SOLERTIA PARUM VULGARI, INDAGAVIT,
SI NON ET INVENIT.
THEOLOGIA QUAM VOCANT CASUUM VERSATISSIMUS
CONSCIENTIIS TURBATIS PACEM CONCILIAVIT,
ERRORUM TENEBRIS INVOLUTAS
VERITATIS LUCE IRRADIAVIT,
IMPEDITISQUE SCRUPULOS EXEMIT.
COGNITIONE, PRUDENTIA, DICENDI FACULTATE
ECCLESIÆ PASTOR OMNIMODO EVANGELICUS.
MULTOS TAM PRIVATO QUAM PUBLICO MINISTERIO
CHRISTO LUCRIFACTOS PORRO ÆDIFICAVIT,
DONEC QUA AGENDO, QUA PATIENDO,
OMNIBUS EXANTLATIS PRO CHRISTO LABORIBUS
PLACIDAM ASSECUTUS EST IN CHRISTO QUIETEM,
AB EDITIS EDENDISQUE OPERIBUS,
VIRI MAXIMI OPTIMO MONUMENTO
NOMEN REPORTATURUS, UNGUENTO PRETIOSIUS
IPSOQUE CUI INSCRIBITUR MARMORE PERENNIUS,
ANNO ÆRÆ CHRISTIANÆ MDCLXXIX.
ÆTAT LXXX. DIE FEBR. XXIII.

TRANSLATED BY THOMAS GIBBONS, D.D., THUS:—

HERE LIES THE BODY OF
THE REV. THOMAS GOODWIN, D.D.
BORN AT ROLLESBY,
IN THE COUNTY OF NORFOLK.
HE HAD A LARGE AND FAMILIAR ACQUAINTANCE
WITH ANCIENT,
AND, ABOVE ALL,
WITH ECCLESIASTICAL HISTORY.
HE WAS EXCEEDED BY NONE
IN THE KNOWLEDGE OF THE HOLY SCRIPTURES.
HE WAS AT ONCE BLESSED WITH A RICH INVENTION
AND A SOLID AND EXACT JUDGMENT.
HE CAREFULLY COMPARED TOGETHER
THE DIFFERENT PARTS OF HOLY WRIT;
AND WITH A MARVELLOUS FELICITY
DISCOVERED THE LATENT SENSE
OF THE DIVINE SPIRIT
WHO INDITED THEM.
NONE EVER ENTERED DEEPER
INTO THE MYSTERIES OF THE GOSPEL,
OR MORE CLEARLY UNFOLDED THEM
FOR THE BENEFIT OF OTHERS.
THE MATTER, FORM, DISCIPLINE,
AND ALL THAT RELATES
TO THE CONSTITUTION OF A TRUE CHURCH OF CHRIST,
HE TRACED OUT WITH AN UNCOMMON SAGACITY,
IF HE WAS NOT RATHER THE FIRST DIVINE
WHO THOROUGHLY INVESTIGATED THEM.
HE WAS EMINENTLY QUALIFIED,
BY THE LIGHT OF SACRED TRUTH,
TO PACIFY TROUBLED CONSCIENCES,
TO DISPEL THE CLOUDS OF MISTAKE,
AND REMOVE NEEDLESS SCRUPLES
FROM PERPLEXED AND BEWILDERED MINDS.
IN KNOWLEDGE, WISDOM, AND ELOQUENCE,
HE WAS A TRULY CHRISTIAN PASTOR.
IN HIS PRIVATE DISCOURSES,

Translation of Epitaph—contd.

AS WELL AS IN HIS PUBLIC MINISTRY,
HE EDIFIED NUMBERS OF SOULS,
WHOM HE HAD FIRST WON TO CHRIST,
TILL HAVING FINISHED HIS APPOINTED COURSE,
BOTH OF SERVICES AND SUFFERINGS,
IN THE CAUSE OF HIS DIVINE MASTER,
HE GENTLY FELL ASLEEP IN JESUS.
HIS WRITINGS ALREADY PUBLISHED,
AND WHAT ARE NOW PREPARING FOR PUBLICATION,
THE NOBLEST MONUMENTS OF THIS GREAT MAN'S PRAISE,
WILL DIFFUSE HIS NAME IN A MORE FRAGRANT ODOUR
THAN THAT OF THE RICHEST PERFUME,
TO FLOURISH IN THOSE FAR DISTANT AGES,
WHEN THIS MARBLE, INSCRIBED WITH HIS JUST HONOUR,
SHALL HAVE DROPT INTO DUST.

HE DIED FEBRUARY 23D, 1679,
IN THE EIGHTIETH YEAR OF HIS AGE.

CONTENTS

		PAGE
I.	BEHOLD IN THE BEGINNING THE ETERNAL SON OF GOD ALREADY BEARING THE PERSONAGE OF THE SON OF MAN	9
II.	HE EMPTIED HIMSELF	13
III.	JESUS OF NAZARETH AS A BELIEVING MAN	22
IV.	THE SON OF MAN HAD NOT WHERE TO LAY HIS HEAD	29
V.	THE UNSEARCHABLE RICHES OF CHRIST	35
VI.	THIS GREEK WORD $\mu\epsilon\tau\rho\iota o\pi a\theta\epsilon\hat{\iota}\nu$ IS EXCEEDINGLY EMPHATICAL	42
VII.	HIS NAME SHALL BE CALLED WONDERFUL	47
VIII.	I FILL UP THAT WHICH IS BEHIND OF THE SUFFERINGS OF CHRIST	56
IX.	PAUL MADE A SPECTACLE: GREEK AND MARGIN—A THEATRE	67
X.	PAUL'S APOSTOLICAL PHILOSOPHY	78
XI.	PAUL'S HYPERBOLES	89
XII.	VERBA IN RES, AS THAT PHILOSOPHER SAID WHEN HE WAS CONVERTED	97
XIII.	SO THEN	109
XIV.	MOTUS PRIMI NON CADUNT SUB LIBERTATEM	121
XV.	A SQUEEZE OF THE FORBIDDEN FRUIT	132
XVI.	AN OUNCE OF THE GOLDEN CALF	139
XVII.	SQUEEZING OIL OUT OF A FLINT	145

		PAGE
XVIII.	JUDAS HEARD ALL JESUS' SERMONS	155
XIX.	THE WORD WHEN IT IS MIXED WITH FAITH	163
XX.	AN INSTINCT FOR CHRIST	172
XXI.	CONSENT MAKES THE MATCH	182
XXII.	THE PRACTICE OF THE PRESENCE OF CHRIST	191
XXIII.	BLOTTING OUT THE HANDWRITING THAT WAS AGAINST US	202
XXIV.	HUMILITY THROUGH MANY HUMILIATIONS	212
XXV.	YE HAVE NEED OF PATIENCE	221
XXVI.	I	231
XXVII.	OUR LORD'S NEW COMMANDMENT: WHAT IS REQUIRED IN IT AND WHAT IS FORBIDDEN IN IT	242
XXVIII.	WHO BELITTLES THE DISEASE BELITTLES THE DOCTOR	252

THOMAS GOODWIN

I

BEHOLD IN THE BEGINNING THE ETERNAL SON OF GOD ALREADY BEARING THE PERSONAGE OF THE SON OF MAN

"CLIMB up to the supremest top and most towering pinnacle of eternity," says Thomas Goodwin, "and you will see the Father pitching upon that particular man Jesus of Nazareth, and already by election and predestination and grace uniting Him to His eternal Son, so as to make of God's Son and of Mary's son, taken together, one God-Man, and so constituting Him and commissioning Him to be the Creator and the Redeemer and the Heir and the Lord of all created things in heaven and on earth." And thus it has come about that this world of ours is at once so divine and so human. So divine in its immeasurable antiquity, in its wonderful constitution and construction, and in its boundless riches of all kinds. As Solomon has it, "Wisdom hath builded her house, she hath hewn out the seven pillars thereof." And as Isaiah has it, "Who but your

Redeemer, O Zion, hath measured the waters in the hollow of His hand, and meted out heaven with the span, and comprehended the dust of the earth in a measure, and weighed the mountains in scales, and the hills in a balance? Who hath done all these omnipotent things but the Good Shepherd of Israel?" And then, when he was writing on the greatest of all subjects to the speculative and philosophical Colossians the Apostle said, "By Him were all things in heaven and earth created, and by Him all created things consist." That is to say, just as He created all things at the first, even so He continues to keep all created things in existence still. But for His conserving hold of them all created things would immediately reel and stagger and dissolve away back into all their original imbecility and nothingness. It is His God-man hand alone that holds all created things in all their present stability and security and excellent order and co-operation. "By Him all things consist." "The Son of God," says Augustine, "did not make the world and depart and leave it to itself." On this same subject our own so philosophical and so evangelical Halyburton has this when he is relating some of the successive steps of his conversion and sanctification and illumination. "Sometimes the God-man would let me see glimpses of His glory even in His works of creation and conservation. Sometimes the heavens declared the glory of their Creator to me, and the firmament showed itself to me as His handywork. Till I could look with real satisfaction of mind and heart upon both the heavens and the earth, and could plainly see the print of His hands upon them all." Now, my brethren, has your conversion and sanctification and mine worked out at all in that way, and do we see, and delight to see, the print of the God-man's hands upon the heavens and the earth? If not, why not? If not, there must surely be something greatly awanting in our conversion and sanctification. For, the highest use and the chief end of all created things is to reveal the God-man to us, and to enable us to rejoice with Him and with all His true saints in the work of His hands. The things we hear and see and touch and treat with and live by every hour of the day: the air we breathe, the food we eat, the water we drink, the clothes we put on, the coal, the iron, the gold, the silver, the oil-wells, the medicine wells—whence came they all? Did they all come into existence by chance? Did they all create and arrange themselves of themselves for our use and service? Hear, O heavens, and give ear, O earth: I have nourished and brought up children, and they have said there is no God. The ox knoweth his owner, and the ass his master's crib, but Israel doth not know, my people do not consider.

"Immediately after my conversion God's excellency began to appear to me in everything: in the sun, in the moon, in the stars, in the waters, and in all nature. The Son of God created this world for this very end, to communicate to us through it a certain image of His own excellency, so that when we are delighted with flowery meadows and gentle breezes we may see in all that only the sweet benevolence of Jesus Christ. When we behold the fragrant rose and the snow-white lily we are to see His love and His purity. Even so the green trees, and the song of birds, what are they but the emanation of His infinite joy and benignity? The crystal rivers, and the murmuring streams, what are they but the footsteps of His favour and grace and beauty? When we behold the brightness of the sun, and the golden edges of the evening cloud, and the beauteous rainbow spanning the whole heaven, we but behold some adumbration of His goodness and His glory. And without any doubt, this is the reason that Christ is called the Sun of Righteousness, the Morning Star, the Rose of Sharon, the Lily of the Valley, the Apple Tree among the trees of the wood, a bundle of myrrh, a doe, and a young hart. But we see the most proper image of Jesus Christ when we behold the intellectual and spiritual beauty of the mind and the heart of a truly holy man." So far Jonathan Edwards, " the greatest mind since Aristotle."

II

HE EMPTIED HIMSELF

FOR once, and in the words "He made Himself of no reputation," our admirable Authorised Version is altogether wrong and the Revised Version is altogether right. It is adorably true indeed that the Eternal Son made Himself of no reputation. Yes; but He did far more than that. He did infinitely far more than that. Paul's great Greek original, ἑαυτὸν ἐκένωσε, if it were correctly and adequately rendered, would run somewhat thus: Who, being in the form of God, thought it no robbery to be equal with God. And yet, for our salvation, HE EMPTIED HIMSELF. That is to say, the Eternal Son despoiled and depleted Himself of all His divine power and heavenly glory, and was made flesh, and was made sin, and became obedient unto death, even the death of the cross.

> His greatness He for us abas'd,
>   For us His glory vail'd;
> In human likeness dwelt on earth,
>   His majesty conceal'd.

What all that divine power and heavenly glory

was which the Eternal Son possessed before He emptied Himself neither the tongue nor the pen even of an inspired apostle can ever attain to tell. But there were some things that the Eternal Son performed in the service of His Father before He emptied Himself: some things that come perhaps somewhat more within the range of revelation and within the scope of the human mind. As thus: "In the beginning was the Word, and the Word was with God, and the Word was God. The same was in the beginning with God. All things were made by Him: and without Him was not anything made that was made. . . . For by Him were all things created that are in heaven, and that are in earth: visible and invisible, all things were created by Him, and for Him, and by Him all things consist."

But wonderful and glorious as all that is, at the same time it had been better that the Son of God had never created this world of ours at all unless He was prepared to do far more for our world than merely to create it and to sustain it in its created existence. For, whatever any of His Father's other worlds might need and might receive at the Son's almighty hands over and above their first creation and their continual preservation, it was divinely foreseen from eternity—nay, the apostle is bold enough to say that it was divinely foreordained from eternity—that sin should enter this world of ours, and with sin, and as its wages, both death and hell. And thus it was that before the foundations of this world of ours were ever laid, the Eternal Father had already committed it to His Eternal Son that, for our salvation from sin and death and hell, He must, in the fulness of time, empty Himself and take upon Himself the form of a servant, and become obedient unto death, even the death of the cross.

And thus it was that when the fulness of time had come, God sent forth His Son, made of a woman, made under the law, to redeem them that were under the law, that we might receive the adoption of sons. And thus it came about that He who had created this world of ours descended into it, and made Himself one of His own earthly creatures, and lived all His appointed time on earth in all the emptiness and limitation and dependence and subjection that was involved in His great work which he had undertaken to perform for His Father. And let it be fully acknowledged here that even the English mistranslation of the true Greek text has its great use to us and reads its great lesson to us. For it is wholly true and it is wholly due to Him that it should be told us concerning our Saviour that He made Himself of no reputation. The whole heavens and the whole earth had all resounded with His great reputation as soon as He had finished the formation of the heavens and the earth and all the host of them. On the seventh day of creation the Son of God ended His great work which He had created and made, and He blessed the seventh day and sanctified it. And on that first Sabbath day all the morning stars sang together before Him, and all the sons of God shouted for joy in His presence. But when the predestinated time for the Son's humiliation and for our salvation came He arose and descended down from His Father's house and left all His heavenly renown and reputation behind Him. And then, as the great prologue has it, He was in the world, and the world was made by Him, and the world knew Him not. He came unto His own, and His own received Him not. How His own received Him, and what entertainment He had at their hands, we read with unspeakable shame and pain on every page of the four Gospels. At the same time all that was no surprise to Him; neither did the reception that He received on this earth take Him at all unawares. From the beginning he had foreseen it all, and had prepared Himself for it all. "Lo, I come. In the volume of the book it is all written of Me." He means that such things as these were written of Him: such awful things as these: "I am a worm, and no man. I am a reproach of men, and despised of the people. All they that see me laugh me to scorn. They shoot out the lip, they shake the head." The Son of God foresaw Himself as in a glass in that awful twenty-second Psalm. Again, this was written, and He had often read it: "He hath no form nor comeliness: and when we shall see Him there is no beauty that we should desire Him." And again, He foresaw that all this also would be written concerning Him, and He had often in anticipation read it: "Then Pilate took Jesus and scourged Him. And the soldiers platted a crown of thorns and put it on His head. And they put on Him a purple robe, and bowed the knee, and said, Hail! King of the Jews. And they smote Him in His face with their hands." Yes, indeed: the Eternal Son, the Maker of the heavens and the earth, made Himself of no reputation! And that one word, of no reputation, mistranslation as it is, makes us sinful men to stop and think. For, how we all live and labour for a reputation! How we are all puffed up with our reputation when it comes to us! And how we are all cast down when our reputation departs from us! But how different from all that was our Divine Lord. O reputation-loving men! in all your ambitions remember your Divine Redeemer. And determine to follow Him henceforth in all His footsteps of self-humiliation. And, like Him, always seek the praise and the reputation that come from God and from a good conscience alone.

But to proceed. Such was His self-depletion that, Divine Sovereign and Divine Lawgiver as He was, He took upon Him the form of a servant, and became obedient to all men in all things. And to begin with, He became obedient to Joseph and Mary in all things and at all times. At twelve years old He went down from His first Passover and was subject to them. And that was so because He humbled Himself to come under the law of a true and proper human childhood. Year after year he lived under the fifth commandment of the Decalogue like any other dutiful son in the house of Israel. So much was this the case, that if you go back and enter Mary's humble home you will see

B

her first-born son making Himself subject to her, and to His brothers and sisters, in everything. He learned obedience by the things that He suffered every day at all their hands. And if you go back and enter Joseph's toilsome workshop you will see Him who had made all things in heaven and on earth now making Himself obedient in cutting and planing wood, and in all joining and mortising work, like any other obedient apprentice in the workshops of Nazareth. "St Joseph was dead, and Jesus had succeeded to His foster-father's modest business." As Dr. Newman has it: "Our Divine Lord was found of no reputation in this world, whether on the score of rank or of education. It seems almost irreverent to speak of His temporal employment; but it is profitable to remind ourselves that the Son of God Himself was a sort of smith, and made ploughs and cattle yokes." Yes, and all the time He never once hinted at what He might have spoken out but for His absolute and ever-silent humility. He never once said to his fellow-workmen what He had found written concerning Himself in the prophet Isaiah: He so hid all these amazing things in His wholly self-emptied and utterly humble heart. "He hath measured the waters in the hollow of His hand, and meted out heaven with the span, and comprehended the dust of the earth in a measure, and weighed the mountains in scales, and the hills in a balance. His own hands hath made all these things." Not that His human hands, born of Mary, had made all these things. No. But without His

Divine Hands, begotten of God, not one of all these things had ever been made. Such and so great was His self-emptiness and His submissiveness and His obedience toward all His earthly tutors and governors. And much more was He submissive and obedient in all things toward His Father in heaven. For, never once, as a child, or as a growing youth, or as a grown-up man, never once was He disobedient to the letter or to the spirit of any part of His Father's holy law ; never once in thought or word or deed. Never once did His conscience make Him a coward. Never once, for a moment, night nor day, did He lose the light of His Father's countenance. No, never once, from Nazareth to Gethsemane. "This is My well-beloved Son, in whom I am well pleased : hear ye Him."

"Wherefore God hath also highly exalted Him." His God and Father had seen all that from His Son's first undertaking of all that down to His finishing of all that. His God and Father had kept in His bottle every tear that His Son the Man of Sorrows had shed during the whole of His sojourn in this world of sorrows. Not one sigh of His, not one sob, not one heavenward breath of secret self-surrendering prayer had escaped His Father's ever-open ear. "And He shall be mine," said His Father, "in that day when I make up My jewels." And it was so, and it now is so, and it shall for ever be so. For all the Divine Son's self-emptiness is for ever at an end now. "Father, the hour is come. Glorify Thy Son, that Thy Son also may glorify Thee. Glorify Thou Me with the glory I had with

Thee before the world was, and before I emptied Myself and was made flesh." And it was so. "Wherefore God hath highly exalted Him, and hath set Him again at His own right hand, far above all principality and power and every name that is named. As it was in the beginning, as it is now, and as it shall for ever be, world without end." And all that to the glory of God the Father. All that to His glory who so loved the world that He gave His only begotten Son to death, even the death of the cross.

Yes, my believing brethren, yes. God's great love accounts for it all. God's everlasting love explains it all. God is love, and that is the true explanation and the sufficient key to it all. Given that God is love, and that God's Eternal Son is God with His Father, and is ever in His Father's bosom: given all that, and all the rest follows as by a Divine necessity. Yes, my loving brethren, you have the true secret and the full explanation of the self-emptying and the humiliation of the cross in your own loving hearts. All you who are born of God, all you who truly love God and one another, all you who greatly love and are greatly loved—in all that you possess in your own bosoms the true explanation and the true key to the whole mystery of redemption, the explanation and the key to that love which passes all explanation and every key. And, after the glory of God, it is to kindle ever afresh the life of a true brotherly love in our hearts that this apostle so carries our hearts captive to the astounding love of Christ toward us. It is to banish for ever from among us all envy of one another, all jealousy of one another, all suspicion of one another, and all strife as to who shall be counted the greatest. It is to make all self-seeking and all vain-glory to be for ever impossible among all Christian men. It is to make us to look not at our own things alone, but every man to look on the honour, and the prosperity, and the whole happiness of other men also. It is on the ground of the amazing and all-conquering love of Christ that the apostle reasons with us, and says to us: "If there be therefore any consolation in Christ: if any comfort of love: if any fellowship of the Spirit: if any bowels and mercies: be ye like-minded, having the same love, being of one accord, of one mind. Let nothing be done through strife and vain-glory, but in lowliness of mind let each esteem other better than themselves. Do all things without murmurings and disputings, that ye may be blameless and harmless: the sons of God without rebuke." In one word, and in a word beyond which even an inspired apostle cannot go: "Let this mind be in you which was also in Christ Jesus, who emptied Himself and humbled Himself even to the death of the cross."

III

JESUS OF NAZARETH AS A BELIEVING MAN

TO begin with, the child Jesus was born of a believing woman. For if there ever was a believing woman on the face of the earth it was surely the Virgin Mary. Never since women were had any woman such things to believe concerning herself and concerning her son as the Virgin Mary was called on to believe. Thou shalt bear a son, and thou shalt call His name Jesus, for He shall save His people from their sins. Then said Mary, how shall this ever be to me? And the angel said, With God nothing is impossible. And Mary said, Behold the handmaiden of the Lord. Be it unto me according to thy word. And it was so, till, as the proverb has it, the child Jesus drank in faith with His mother's milk. And till, as Dante has it, "Hers was the face that unto His had most resemblance."

"It may safely be affirmed," says Thomas Goodwin, "that as soon as the understanding of the child Jesus began to put forth any acts of reason, His heart began at the same time as good as to believe. There was in Mary's first-born son a natural instinct, an aboriginal tendency of spirit toward everything that was good, and God-ward, and heaven-ward. That spiritual law of holy believing which was to rule every hour of His after-life began from His first intelligence to carry all things along with it, just as the *primum mobile* in the heavens carries along with it all the rest of the spheres." And thus it was that the child Jesus took so early to Joseph's family worship, and to Joseph's family Bible, as you will sometimes see well-born children do among ourselves. From a child Jesus knew the Holy Scriptures in all their profitableness for doctrine and for instruction in righteousness till that Man of God was made perfect, being thoroughly furnished unto all good works. But with all that it took Him till He began to be about thirty years of age to achieve for Himself both the name and the place of the author and finisher of our faith. It was during the hidden years of His early manhood that Jesus was led of the Spirit to discover and to receive and to believe and fully to accept all that was written in Moses and in David and in Isaiah concerning Himself. Try to think of Jesus of Nazareth, the carpenter's son, as He read and read day and night, and weekday and Sabbath-day, all the Messianic Scriptures that had been written in the volume of the Book concerning Himself, and concerning no other man in all the world but Himself. Just try to think of Him as He read a thousand times now the twenty-second Psalm, and now the fortieth Psalm, and now the fifty-third chapter of Isaiah. Look at Him as He closes the terrible Book and takes refuge from it in His hard day's work. And look at Him as soon as His hard day's work is over, again taking up the terrible Book and going away with it to a mountain top apart, there to read and to ponder and to pray till He was somewhat able to receive and to believe and to submit to what He continually read. A thousand times He read those awful Messianic passages through His sweat and His tears, till He again received strength, and faith, and resignation and surrender to say, Thy will be done. I do not wonder that it took Mary's first-born Son a whole thirty years of faith, and prayer, and spiritual conflict to take home to Himself the astounding work that He had been chosen and foreordained and predestinated of His Father to perform for God and man. The wonder rather is that He was ever able to receive and to realise and to accept that He, and not another, was to be the Messiah of Israel and the Redeemer of all mankind.

Our Lord's sin-atoning work is almost more clearly and more circumstantially written out in the Old Testament than it is even in the New Testament. And that is so, as I apprehend, for this sufficient reason. The Old Testament is so circumstantially full of the atonement, both in written prophecy and in acted ritual, because it was to be put into the hand of Jesus of Nazareth to be His great key to all His so mysterious life on earth, and then to the awful mystery of his sin-atoning death. It cannot be said indeed that the whole of the Old Testament was written for Jesus' sake alone. No. But it is the simple truth to say that it was all written for the instruction and for the faith and for the guidance and for the holy obedience of Jesus of Nazareth, far more than for all its other readers taken together. And as the Man Jesus of Nazareth, the carpenter's son, lived and laboured through those thirty years: and as He read and read and read, now concerning His eternal election to the office of our Redeemer, and now concerning the reception He was to meet with in Jerusalem, and now concerning Gethsemane and Calvary, unless His Heavenly Father's superabounding grace and strength had held Him up our Saviour would surely have gone beside Himself with what He so clearly foresaw concerning Himself. But He so received from His Father the spirit of faith and love and hope and full assurance that when He began to be about thirty years of age He was able to take His stand beside the altar in the temple and to say with His whole heart, Lo, I come, in the volume of the Book it is written of Me, I delight to do Thy will, yea, Thy law is written in My heart.

But contemporaneous with all our Lord's absolutely unparalleled trials of faith and patience during those thirty preparatory years, there were daily and hourly trials and triumphs of faith and patience much more like some of our own daily trials and triumphs. I have often wondered at the severe silence of the four Gospels concerning the everyday life of our Lord during those thirty disciplinary and preparatory years in Nazareth. But though it has seemed good to the Holy Ghost and to the four Evangelists that the veil should hang so close over all those thirty years, even so, our wondering and worshipping eyes do sometimes see some momentary tremblings and upliftings of that secret veil. There is one very painful thing of which we have only too good evidence. And that is the great uncongenialness and unhappiness of His home life. There is a parenthentical verse in John's Gospel that always makes my heart bleed as often as I read it or recall it. *Neither did His brethren believe in Him.* What a life of loneliness and pain and shame and sorrow untold lies hidden behind those two or three words of the Evangelist concerning his Master's home life! What a solace and what a strength it would have been to Him in His life of such faith and such forecast had He been happy at home! But He was always alone, and much worse than alone, in His mother's house. For, absolutely unaccountable, and absolutely impossible, as it seems to us, His very mother herself was carried away, sometimes, with the unbelief and the disrespect and the disloyalty to Him of all her other children. But all things work together for good to them that love God, to them who are the called according to His purpose. And thus it was that all our Lord's want of sympathy and love and honour at home, all that but the more drove Him back upon His Bible and upon prayer, and upon more constant communion with His Father in heaven. And till He had all those Old Testament Scriptures by heart where such things as these are written : He hath put my brethren far from me, and mine acquaintances are turned strange to me. My kinsfolk have failed me, and my familiar friends have forgotten me. They that dwell in the same house with me count me for a stranger, and I am an alien in their eyes. Can a woman forget her sucking child, that she should not have compassion on the son of her womb ? Yea, they may forget, yet will I not forget Thee. I can hear Him repeating these and many such like scriptures to Himself, as He worked in Joseph's carpentering and dwelt in His mother's house.

Then, again, even after He was sealed and sent out as the promised Messiah, even so, He had many sore trials of faith to endure and many great downcasting and distressing experiences in connection with His teaching and preaching. Sometimes, indeed, the whole land seemed to be moved by His sermons. There were times when the largest synagogues overflowed and when the surrounding streets were filled with the pressing crowds that gathered round His pulpit. But again the tide of His attractiveness and popularity receded, till He was left all but alone. The common people heard Him gladly so long as He preached to them in homely household parables and wove interesting anecdotes into his sermons. But when His preaching became personal and spiritual and inward and experimental, as in the sixth of John, from that time the fluctuating crowds dissolved and dispersed and left Him all but alone. And at such seasons of disappointment and defeat His faith in the success of

His ministry and His hope of ever teaching spiritual truth to such an unspiritual people sometimes sank very low. It was on one of those depressed and dejected occasions that Peter so strengthened and cheered his Master. Our Lord was in all points tempted and tried like all His believing brethren: but, especially, like all His believing brethren in the ministry of the divine Word. And thus it is that, from time to time, He sends hearers like Peter to cheer and reassure their ministers amid their manifold disappointments and defeats and dejections of heart.

But all the former strains and tests that had been put upon Jesus' faith were as nothing compared with the tremendous strain and test of Gethsemane and Calvary. Though He slay me, yet will I trust in Him, said Job. The man of Uz both spoke and acted splendidly in the day of his great trial and tribulation. But at his best Job was only a far-off forerunner of our Lord. For what was but a bold hypothesis and a powerful hyperbole in Job came to be a terrible reality in the case of Jesus of Nazareth. Till about the ninth hour Jesus cried with a loud voice, My God, My God, why hast Thou forsaken Me? Father, into Thy hands I commit My spirit. And when He had received the vinegar, He said, It is finished, and gave up the ghost. Now, who is among you that feareth the Lord: that obeyeth the voice of His servant: that walketh in darkness, and hath no light, let him trust in the Name of the Lord, and stay his heart upon his God.

IV

THE SON OF MAN HAD NOT WHERE TO LAY HIS HEAD

IT was not fitting that our Lord should have a house and a household of His own in this world. It was not expedient that He should be other than a stranger and a pilgrim on this earth as so many of His brethren in all ages have been and still are. All the same, it somewhat startles us when Goodwin says that our Lord "lived on pure charity," every day and every hour for the last three years of His life. But that is just another way of saying what our Lord said Himself. The foxes have holes, He said, and the birds of the air have nests: but the Son of Man hath not where to lay His head. Before we begin to realise what we read in the Gospels we say, What! Did He not always have His mother's house? Was His mother's door not always open to her son all His days? And would He not have been made welcome to have come back as often as He liked? But, so far as we are told, He never once came back to Joseph's workshop nor to Mary's fireside after He had once been separated to the Gospel.

Not thinking of what we say we talk of " the holy family " in Nazareth. But it was very far from being a holy family, at any rate as long as our Lord lived and prayed and waited for its slow-coming holiness. It was Martha's family at Bethany that both earned and deserved that happy name. As if He was thinking of Martha and Mary and Lazarus our homeless Lord said on one occasion, the same is My mother and sister and brother. No. He was not speaking poetically nor rhetorically, but rather with a sore and a heavy heart, when He said that the foxes had holes and the birds of the air had nests. And He must often have said that to Himself, not bitterly, but obediently and submissively, when, after His hard day's work in the city, and when it was too late, or when He was too tired to go out to Bethany, He went out to spend the night on the Mount of Olives. With his eye on the object Goodwin says : " In this place Christ used often to rest and to pray. For when He saw that He was to die, and that now His time was come, He wore His body out. He cared not, as it were, what became of Him ; He was good enough for the cross. And, therefore, He wholly spent Himself in praying and preaching and other work. Sometimes He spent the whole night in prayer privately, and sometimes He took His disciples with Him."

" He came to His own, and His own received Him not." It is not meant that they did not receive Him sometimes into their houses. It is not meant that they never spread a pillow on which He was to lay His head. No. But the much more sad meaning is this—

HE HAD NOT WHERE TO LAY HIS HEAD 31

that they did not receive Him and His grace and truth into their minds and hearts : especially the truth as it is in Jesus. It was this that made Him so homeless and such a stranger all His days in His mother's house. There is nothing, my brethren, in the New Testament so hard to be understood to me as His mother's house. Had Mary never told His brothers and His sisters about the conception and the birth of their elder brother ? Or, was it of her that the prophet spake—she may forget ? Had she lived in such an atmosphere of unbelief and disesteem and rejection and scorn for thirty years that, even after all she had come through, she sometimes came to take sides against Him, and to become another unbeliever like the rest of them ? You know yourselves how a life spent among unbelievers and scoffers tends to sap away all your own best belief, till sometimes you almost disbelieve your own best existence, and even the existence of your own God and Saviour. And do you not feel sure that it was of such as you are that He was thinking when He said, If any man will come after Me, let him take up his cross daily at home and follow Me ? For He was in all points made like unto His tempted and tried brethren, especially at home. At any rate, as often as we think of His mother's house, let us bless the name of Martha and of her sister Mary, and their believing and beloved brother Lazarus, concerning whom the Holy Ghost has had it written : " The Word was in the world, and the world was made by Him, and the world knew Him not. But as many as received Him to them gave He power to become the sons of God, even to them that believed in His Name."

Now, with all that, the one question for the writer and the reader of these lines is this: Have we received and retained increasingly in our minds and in our hearts the grace and the truth of God as they are revealed and offered in Jesus Christ? Has He where to lay His head and His heart in us? Is His saving Name far above every other name in heaven and earth to us? Can we honestly sing with John Newton, and say, How sweet the Name of JESUS sounds! If we are preachers, have we said to our people what Paul said to the Corinthians: I am determined not to know anything among you save Jesus Christ, and Him crucified. And again to the Galatians: God forbid that I should glory, save in the cross of our Lord Jesus Christ, whereby the world is crucified unto me, and I unto the world. And with Richard Hooker when he is full of Paul's mind : " Let it be counted folly, or phrenzy, or fury, or whatsoever. It is our wisdom, and our comfort; we care for no knowledge in the world but this, that man hath sinned, and God hath suffered : that God hath made Himself the sin of men, and that men are made the righteousness of God."

Butler is always warning us not to let our strong emotions pass off without adequate actions. Now, in this case when our hearts are touched with the

HE HAD NOT WHERE TO LAY HIS HEAD

feeling of our Redeemer's poverty, let us immediately turn our emotions into something actual and practical. And if our Lord does not any more need a supper and a bed, others do who are as dear to Him as if they were Himself. And, speaking of them to the Marthas and Marys who stand on His right hand at the last day He is to say : Inasmuch as you did it to My poor in your day, you did it to Me. As I write I see the Misses Mackenzie of our Moray Place standing beside Martha and Mary when He says to them all that He has told us He will certainly say. Number 16 Moray Place was a perfect Bethany as long as the Misses Mackenzie occupied it. It was not a small house, but it was always full from floor to attic of aged and infirm ministers come in to see the doctor, and decayed missionaries on furlough, and poor students from Waldensia and Moravia who had come to the New College to study, and who had not elsewhere to lay their head. The two Edinburgh sisters are now with the two Bethany sisters. Who in Edinburgh is taking their hospitable place, or is henceforth resolved to take it?

But after all that, there is a previous question. Have we opened our door to Christ Himself? And, if not to Himself in the body, then have we opened it to Himself in the Spirit? Has He knocked at the door of our heart, and have we opened the door, till He has come in and supped with us and we with Him? And is He always welcome to our heart and our house at all hours of the day and night? When a much-loved and a long-expected friend knocks at our door we know his knock and we open the door and say to him, Even so, come quickly. We say, Come away, for I was just thinking about you when you knocked. I was just reading one of your old letters to occupy myself till you should knock. I could not sleep last night for dreaming about you; come away, come away. Sit up in that way for Him to-night. Expect Him this very night. Set a candle in your window for Him to-night. Have your door ajar for Him to-night. And that is said, not to former friends of His only, but it is said to all manner of men. For these are His own words to you to-night: " If ANY MAN hear My voice, and open the door, I will come in to him, and will sup with him, and he with Me." Remember the Gospel words, ANY MAN. It was a proverb in Athens that he was always full of all elasticity and all affability who had supped last night with Plato.

V

THE UNSEARCHABLE RICHES OF CHRIST

IN a letter which is to be read in the classical Cardiphonia collection John Newton tells Thomas Scott this story. A much valued ministerial friend of his, for many years after his ordination, was a complete rationalist toward all divine things. But one day as he was reading his Greek Testament he came on the Greek word which is rendered "unsearchable" in the third chapter of Paul's Epistle to the Ephesians. And immediately his thoughts were powerfully arrested by that wonderful expression of the Apostle. And as he reflected over that wonderful expression he said to himself that Paul employs some very wonderful words in all this wonderful chapter. He speaks, for instance, of what are to him "unsearchable riches" where I find nothing unsearchable at all. He speaks also of heights and depths and lengths and breadths where I find everything plain and simple and easy. Now, what can such a man as the Apostle possibly mean by all these so strong and so unparalleled expressions? And that reflection led Newton's friend to a searching examination of the whole of Paul's Epistles. An examination that ended in a total change both of his personal religion and of all his ministerial work—pulpit and pastoral. The whole story is told in Newton's Seventh Letter to Scott, and after another letter of the same kind Newton had the happiness of seeing Scott taking his stand beside himself as a spiritually-minded and an evangelical minister of the Pauline Gospel. And now, arrested ourselves by that same wonderful expression, "the unsearchable riches of Christ," let us give ourselves up this communion morning to the consideration of Jesus Christ in the matter of His unsearchable riches.

And, first, let us reflect on the unsearchable riches we possess simply in our possession of Christ Himself. For Christ simply in Himself is an infinitely greater possession than all the creation and providential and even redemption riches that we possess in Him. As the famous Puritan aphorism has it, *aliquid in Christo formosius salvatore.* That is to say, there is far more riches in Christ when He is simply taken by Himself, than there is in His being our Saviour. For, long before He became our Saviour, in the beginning was the Word, and the Word was with God, and the Word was God. All things were made by Him, and without Him was not anything made that was made. Which unsearchable revelation in John's Gospel, when taken along with God's unsearchable revelation of His Divine Son in Paul,—when taken together show us something of what God's Son was before He became our Saviour. It was such great scriptures as John's Gospel and Paul's Epistles that led Thomas Goodwin to say concerning John and Paul that "strong swimmers seek deep waters." Yes; there are unsearchable riches in the Divine Sonship of Christ past all finding out even by those who have been enabled to see deepest into the Divine mystery of Jesus Christ. And, then, time and space, as we call them, and all that they contain, were made by Him. As Paul has it, by Him were all things created that are in heaven and that are in earth, visible and invisible, all things were created by Him and for Him; and not only were the unsearchable riches of the coming Gospel hid in God from ages and from generations, but the unsearchable riches of creation also were equally hidden with Christ in God. And just as the unsearchable riches of the Gospel were in the fulness of time revealed to the Apostles, and through them to the Church, somewhat so has it been with the unsearchable riches of creation. And just as many Old Testament prophets and righteous men greatly desired to see those Gospel riches that we now see, so has it been with the riches of creation. From Moses down to Solomon, and from Solomon down to "the secretary of creation," as Dante called Aristotle, and from Aristotle down to our own Newton and Darwin, the noble and fruitful search into the riches of creation has gone on to our great enrichment and to God's great glory. Long ago David sang this noble creation song :—

> The heavens God's glory do declare,
> The skies His hand-work preach;
> Day utters speech to day, and night
> To night doth knowledge teach.
> There is no speech nor tongue to which
> Their voice doth not extend;
> Their line has gone through all the earth,
> Their words to the world's end.

David sang the psalm and Isaiah preached the sermon, as thus: "Who hath measured the waters in the hollow of His hand, and meted out heaven with the span, and comprehended the dust of the earth in a measure, and weighed the mountains in scales, and the earth in a balance? Lift up your eyes on high, and behold who created all these things, that bringeth forth their host by number: He calleth them all by their names by the greatness of His might, for that He is strong in power not one faileth." "The light thus kindled," says Thomas Halyburton, "He daily increased to me: and He confirmed me more and more by ever new discoveries of Himself. Till I could look with satisfaction upon the heavens and the earth and could see the print of His hands upon them all."

"All things were made by Him, and by Him all things consist." That is to say, all created things continue to hold together and to work together to the glory of their Creator and Preserver, and to their enjoyment of Him, and of one another in Him. Athanasius is very clear and cogent on this as he is on everything that he touches. These are some of his characteristic words on this great matter. "From

THE UNSEARCHABLE RICHES OF CHRIST 39

the Divine Father and Fountainhead of all Life and all Love the Divine Son came forth to create all things, and He continues to keep all created things in harmonious existence and co-operation. And the reason of that is truly admirable and is in every way most befitting. For the essential nature of all the creatures is dissoluble and feeble and mortal. But on the other hand, their Creator and Preserver is full of all goodness and life and strength and order and beauty. And lest the creation should dissolve and reel back into its original nothingness, He upholds it, and sustains it, and governs it every moment of its existence. That is to say, by Christ their creator all things consist. In Christ as in a Divine Root. The whole creation is engrafted so as to live together in Him and work together in Him to everlasting."

So far the greatest of the Greek Fathers.

But absolutely unsearchable as the riches of Christ were and are, both in Himself and in His divine offices of Creation and Providence, at the same time things had come to such a pass with mankind that it had been better they had never been either created or preserved unless they were to be redeemed, renewed, and sanctified; recreated indeed, and preserved to the life everlasting. And hence it is that the unsearchable riches of Christ as our Redeemer concerns us so absorbingly here this morning. And thus, magnificent as the Apostle is, first on Christ in Himself, and then on His offices of creation and providence, even so, it is to Christ crucified that Paul determines to give up the whole of his great evangelical Epistles. And it is this that makes us read Paul's great evangelical Epistles till we have taste left for little or nothing else. Our needs as sinners are simply unsearchable. Every new day discovers to us anew how absolutely unsearchable and indescribable are our needs as sinners. But, then, over against all our absolutely unsearchable and indescribable needs as sinners, God is continually setting the far more unsearchable and indescribable riches of His Son as our Saviour. Till as life goes on with us we more and more see that, desperate as our case is, yet we are only all that the more complete in Christ. And that discovery, that experience, once really begun will go on till we are translated to discover and to experience still more and more of Christ's unsearchable riches in His Father's heavenly kingdom.

Now, all that about Christ and His glory in creation and in redemption will make some communicants only the more to stagger and shrink back from the Lord's Table. Some communicants will say that their sinfulness is so unsearchable that they tremble to approach the holy elements. Yes, my brethren, you are right in that, your sinfulness is far more unsearchable than you have yet seen, or will believe. But all the same, however unsearchable your sinfulness is, Christ is infinitely more unsearchable as your Saviour. For your encouragement just look back at the first Lord's Table. What a company of the chief of sinners sat around their

Saviour that night in the upper room! Look at the two disciples whom He loved most, and for whom He had done most. For they are the very disciples who but yesterday had broken His heart by their despicable disputes as to who should be the greatest. Till, full of pain and shame at their disgraceful behaviour, He poured water into a bason and washed their wicked feet. And, more than that, we would have thought that if that Table was to be absolutely fenced and shut against any man it would be against Judas Iscariot. But no. For such was his Master's unsearchable mercy even toward the traitor that He not only washed his false feet, but actually put the cup of salvation up to his false lips! Oh, if only Judas had cast himself and his thirty pieces of silver at his Saviour's feet at that Table!

Trembling communicant, only believe, and come. For he that cometh will in no wise be cast out. Be not afraid, only believe, and come.

VI

THIS GREEK WORD μετριοπαθεῖν IS EXCEEDINGLY EMPHATICAL

THERE are a dozen renderings offered us of the great Greek word μετριοπαθεῖν (Authorised Version, "have compassion on"; Revised Version, "bear gently with"). But I have never forgotten Dr Thomas Goodwin's rendering of that great Greek word which I came across one Sabbath night when I was at college, more than fifty years ago. And that rendering of the great Puritan, I may almost say, has never been a day out of my mind all these fifty years. How could it?

"This great Greek word," says Thomas Goodwin, " is exceedingly emphatical. It means much more than the English rendering 'who can have compassion' means. For, when this great Greek word of the Apostle is rightly rendered, and is rightly laid to heart, it reveals to us that Jesus Christ, our great High Priest, not only has a great compassion in His heart, but that He has a special and a particular compassion *measured out* according to every individual man's measure of need, according to every individual man's speciality, and particularity, and singularity, and secrecy of need." That is Thomas Goodwin's both grammatical and experimental rendering of this extraordinarily expressive Greek word $\mu\epsilon\tau\rho\iota o\pi a\theta\epsilon\hat{\iota}\nu$. And after going by it for fifty years, I feel to-day more fully assured than ever that his scholarly and experimental and homiletical exegesis gives us the comforting mind of the Holy Spirit far away better than do the comparatively cold and dry renderings of the Authorised and Revised Versions. And the comforting mind of the Spirit, possessing the mind and directing the pen of the Apostle, assures every greatly tempted and tried and afflicted and sorrow-laden soul of man that all his so great and so exceptional sorrows are all well known to his great High Priest, and are laid to heart by Him as if they were His own, as, indeed, they are. And that his great High Priest will most assuredly sympathise with him, and will most assuredly both succour and deliver him to all the exact measure, and speciality, and singularity, and particularity, and absolute secrecy of all his sinfulness and all his sorrowfulness.

Preaching on this same great Greek word to the City Temple congregation of his day, and preaching in all his own incomparably realising and homecoming way, Dr Goodwin spoke as follows: " I need my great High Priest to have not only all the abilities and all the attributes and all the great qualifications that you need in Him; but, over and above all that, I, Thomas Goodwin, your minister, need Him always urgently, and indeed sometimes absolutely agonizingly, for certain special and secret and altogether individual needs of my own; needs of my own that no other mortal man knows anything about, nor would believe even if I confessed them to him; needs of my own that are so exceptionally and so exclusively my own that no other man before me, or now around me, or coming after me, will ever have needs exactly like them. It is absolutely inconceivable to me," he said, "that any other man, past, present, or to come, could ever have just that combination, and just that concentration, and just that incidence of sin and sorrow that I have, together with all the temporal and spiritual intricacies, of all kinds, of which both my heart and my life are brimful. No other man in all this sinful and sorrowful city of London has just my crosses and cups and thorns in his flesh. No man of you all," he said, as he looked down into all their hearts and around into all their homes. "And difficult as it is for me to believe that even my all-perfect Saviour can be the exact second and parallel and double and duplicate of me, yet it is so, and I, with my whole mind and heart, believe that it is so." And it was in scholarly and evangelical and experimental preaching like that that the first foundations of the City Temple were laid, and the foundations also of Thomas Goodwin's own splendid name and lasting fame as an incomparably Pauline and Puritan preacher of Jesus Christ, His person and His work. "A man's own need," says Pascal, "is the measure of his greatness."

Go home, then, as Goodwin was wont to say,

and never after this morning's great Scripture forget that whatsoever trial or temptation or thorn or cross or cup of any kind is in your appointed lot, you have the most absolute assurance that Jesus Christ your great High Priest was at one time placed under the very same trial and temptation and thorn and cross and cup under which you are placed. Or if His was not exactly and absolutely the very same identical trial and temptation and thorn and cross and cup as yours is, then all His trials and temptations were as like yours as the Holy Spirit could possibly make them. And He made them in this way—the Holy Spirit, with the all-seeing eye of the Godhead, and with all the omnipresence of the Godhead, looked down all the generations of God's elect and saw you and singled you out according to your foreordained trials and temptations and thorns and crosses and cups. And then with you in His eye the Holy Spirit returned to His great work on the Man Jesus Christ, and went forward from day to day to make Him after your very image and likeness and exact pattern till like you He was the Man of all kinds of sorrows. And thus it was so divinely and so graciously brought about that, experimentally, as we say, and as Man, Jesus Christ is able to have all possible compassion upon you; while at the same time as God He is able omnisciently and omnipotently to succour you and to deliver you to the uttermost. Yes, poor sorrow-laden soul, to the very uttermost! Go home, then, this morning to all your trials and temptations and thorns and crosses and cups, and among them all, and as long as they last, come boldly every day and every hour to the throne of grace in order to obtain all needed mercy and to find all needed grace in every time of need. For, μετριοπαθεῖν δυνάμενος, your great High Priest is able and is willing and is waiting to have compassion on you according to all the exact measure, and speciality, and particularity, and singularity, and secrecy of all your needs.

Wherefore, holy brethren, partakers of the heavenly calling, consider the Apostle and High Priest of our profession, Jesus Christ. For we are made partakers of Christ if we hold the beginning of our confidence steadfast unto the end.

VII

HIS NAME SHALL BE CALLED WONDERFUL

THE Divine Nature is the most wonderful thing in heaven and our own human nature is the most wonderful thing on earth. But He whose name is Wonderful is far more wonderful than God, while He is at the same time far more wonderful than man. And that is so because He combines and embodies in Himself all the wonderfulness of God along with all the wonderfulness of man. And thus it is that His great name the God-Man is by far the most wonderful of all His names.

"In the beginning was the Word, and the Word was with God, and the Word was God, and the Word was made flesh." Now, next to the amazing wonder of the Word being made flesh, was the amazing wonder of what the Word did to Himself before He was made flesh. For when He made Himself flesh, in the Apostle's wonderful words, He emptied Himself. That is to say, the Divine Word laid down all His Godhead power and glory and blessedness and in the place of all that He took upon Himself thirty-three years of our earthly poverty and labour and homelessness and loneliness, and all manner of our earthly sorrow, till He attained to that wonderful name for Him to bear—the Man of Sorrows. How wonderful that the Maker and the Heir and the Owner of heaven and earth should so impoverish Himself as to have to say that the foxes have holes, and the birds of the air have nests, but the Son of Man hath not where to lay His head. And, as if all that were not wonderful enough, not only was the Son of God made man, but, surely, most amazing of all, He was made sin, till He died for sin the accursed death of the Cross, a death both wonderful and fearful, beyond all words of God or man. No wonder that the elect angels bow down and desire to look into the wonderful mystery of the Incarnation of the Son of God, and then into the awful mystery of the Atonement He made for human sin! And no wonder that the whole of heaven rings to-day with the worship of the Lamb that was slain before the foundation of the world!

But, my brethren, all that, wonderful beyond all words as it is—yet all that is but preliminary and preparatory to the wonderfulness of His name as your Redeemer and mine. For all His Godhead and all His Manhood and all His obedience and all His sin-atoning satisfaction, with all His Highpriesthood in heaven—all that was absolutely necessary before He could say to us this communion morning " Him that cometh to Me I will in no wise cast out," and before it could be preached concerning Him this morning that He is able to save to the uttermost. And indeed it is not till He begins to save us to the uttermost that we become at all truly awake to any part of His wonderfulness, past or present, in heaven or on earth. It is only when we become to ourselves the greatest possible proof of His Divine power and grace to save—it is only then that we begin to go back upon and to dwell upon His Eternal Sonship and His human incarnation and His sin-atoning death and His restored and increased power and glory in heaven.

Well, then, communicants, come away and let me begin with you at the real and true beginning of your wonderful salvation. For you must know that the real and true beginning of your salvation was not when you first communicated; no, nor was it when you first believed. The real and true wonderfulness of your salvation goes much further back than either your regeneration or your conversion, wonderful as those two things were to you and ever will be. For you must know that your salvation goes back for its real and true beginning to that time before time was when the Son of God was Himself chosen and was predestinated to be your Saviour, and when you were chosen and predestinated in Him to be saved by Him. Being who and what He was He was very wonderful in His eternal election and predestination—very, very wonderful. But so were you, in another way, you being not as yet in existence, unless it was in the eternal foreknowledge and purpose and decree of Almighty God. Come then, all intending communicants, and join with the greatest and the best of communicants in His glorious doxology over all that. You all have that glorious doxology by heart: "Blessed be the God and Father of our Lord Jesus Christ, who hath blessed us with all spiritual blessings in heavenly places in Christ: according as He hath chosen us in Him before the foundation of the world, that we should be holy and without blame before Him in love: having predestinated us to the adoption of children by Jesus Christ to Himself: to the praise of the glory of His grace, wherein He hath made us accepted in the Beloved": that to the communicants in Ephesus. And then on the same level this: "To all that be in Rome, beloved of God, and who are the called according to His purpose. For whom He did foreknow He also did predestinate to be conformed to the image of His Son, that He might be the first-born among many brethren." And this to the Thessalonians on the same level: "Brethren, beloved of God, because God hath from the beginning chosen you to salvation through sanctification of the spirit and belief of the truth." And teaching Timothy what to preach at his communion seasons in Ephesus, and how to preach it, Paul writes thus: "Wherefore I put thee in remembrance of the power of God, who hath saved us and hath called us with an holy calling: not according to our worth, but according to His own purpose and grace, which was given us in Christ before the world began." And so Peter, and so all the Apostles when they were taught of God concerning things it had not entered into the heart of mortal man to conceive. All which things, communicants, were not written for your forerunners in Ephesus and in Rome and in Thessalonica and in Asia only, but for you also, if you will but receive them and believe them. Only, to tell you the truth, I have some fear concerning some of you, lest that apostolic doctrine concerning the real and true beginning of your salvation is too strong meat for some of you. Now, in this great matter, just how is it with you? Are any of you such babes at the breast as to be unable to hear such great things as these about the Divine sovereignty and eternal antiquity of your salvation? Would you rather have a few drops of milk this morning than a meal of the marrow of lions? Oh no! Oh no! You must not turn away from the full wonderfulness of your salvation. Not to-day, at any rate. No, not while this Table is still spread. Come, then, all you who are still but weak in the faith : come and let us reason together concerning the greatness of your salvation. But for your eternal election in and with Christ, why else are you here? How else account to us and to yourselves for your being where you now are? Did God the Father choose you to this day, and to all that this day represents and involves, or did you choose Him? Do not mock me, you say. I am far from mocking you, for I am honouring you and exalting you beyond all the wonders and honours of earth and heaven, if you will only believe me, if you will only believe Paul, if you will only believe the Holy Ghost, who inspired Paul. Say this, then, before you enter the Table, say : "Lord, I believe all that ; help Thou mine unbelief."

At this point, and from among a thousand crowding wonders, take this that Paul ventured on in a sederunt he held with the elders of Ephesus; this that they were redeemed with no less a price than the very blood of very God. Do you hear that, O sin-burdened communicant? If you have heard that almost too awful word, then have a full faith in that awful Blood. Have and put forth a full and a strong and an immediate and an abiding and a growing faith in the Blood of the God-Man. When, as now, your sins rise up and stare you in the face, when they are ever before you, then have swift recourse to the Blood of God. And, as Goodwin says: "As your lawyers lay *aqua fortis* upon letters of evil ink to eat them out of their parchments, so still be you adipping the hands of your faith in the Blood of God. This do at every Sacrament time especially, till you have a free and a full access to that peace which passes all understanding." O yes! Wonderful Divine Blood, shed by God the Son for the elders and people of Ephesus and for your elders and you!

And so on, communicants, till ever the closer home you come to yourselves the more wonderful will your Saviour become to you. As thus: Your utter helplessness against your indwelling and insurmountable sinfulness will always throw you back on the absolute Godhead of your Saviour. The thing that made Athanasius stand up against the whole world was his own indwelling and insurmountable sinfulness. "I, for one, must have a Saviour who is absolutely Divine," that great father always insisted: "No creature, the greatest

HIS NAME SHALL BE CALLED WONDERFUL 53

and the best, can ever suffice for me. No one short of Almighty God can ever save me. And since I have begun to experience my Saviour's power to save me, though the whole world should deny His Godhead, I will live and die confessing Him as my Lord and my God." And it is that very same lifelong experience that compels the present preacher to symbolise with that great Greek father. My wound, like his, is far too deep for any physician short of God to heal. And my ever-running sore, like his, is far too foul for any of your rosewaters to wash. Like Athanasius and like Paul I must have blood, and that the Blood of God, till, as I wash in the Blood of Christ, I will always say with Athanasius, and with Paul, and with the once-doubting Thomas, " My Lord and my God ! "

Another most homecoming thing, and at the same time a most overpoweringly wonderful thing, is the omnipresence of Christ with all His people, and with each several one of all His people. The wonderful ubiquity of the Divine Nature is written on every page of the Holy Scriptures; but the omnipresence of Jesus Christ is much more wonderful than that. For, while He is always and everywhere present with us in His wonderful Godhead, He is at the same time always and everywhere present with us in His wonderful Manhood also. It was not as the omnipresent Son of God only that He said to His disciples that He would be always with everyone of them to the end of the world. It was the God-Man who spake to them, and who so speaks to us. My brethren, how wonderful is that! How consoling is that! How strengthening is that! It is far too wonderful for any of us to understand it. But better than understanding it we have the experience and the possession of it. The God-Man knows Himself how He does it. But that He does do it every true believer of His is witness. *Deus ubique est, et totus ubique est;* that was one of Augustine's constant axioms. That is to say, God is everywhere, and He is wholly everywhere. And the God-Man is all that in a still more wonderful way. The God-Man would be wonderful beyond all words to me were He only present with me at all times and in all places and in all circumstances, and that to hear me and to help me and to save me. But by what Name am I to call Him when I think of Him as quite as much present with you as He is with me? And, then, with all and every one of His people in heaven and on earth, as much as He is with you and me. Thomas Halyburton said to us the other Sabbath evening that when he tried to think aright of Christ he was always compelled to bow down before His absolute incomprehensibility. And I thank Halyburton for all he says on that subject. Hooker, also, is simply indispensable upon the omnipresence of Christ. And the Abbot of Buckfast has this in our way: "There is in Christ a kind of multiplicity of spiritual pronouns that makes Him the personal spiritual friend of millions of souls. In His humanity He has for all practical purposes the illimitability of divinity itself." And Walter Marshall: "Though Christ be in heaven and we on earth, yet He can join our souls and bodies to

His at such a distance without any substantial change in either, by the same infinite Spirit dwelling in Him and in us."

But, my brethren, after all that the greatest theologians and the greatest preachers can say about the wonderfulness of our Lord and Saviour Jesus Christ, every saved sinner will have his own special and unshared experience of that wonderfulness till he will have his own everlasting song concerning it. And it will take all that multitude which no man can number, to all eternity to tell out before the Father the half of the whole wonderfulness of His eternal and incarnate Son. Some of you will think this morning that no one in the whole heaven will be able to tell of all His wonderfulness like you. Yes! but that is just what I always think. I always think of myself as saying to David, and to Isaiah, and to Peter, and to the Magdalene, and to the publican, and to the thief, and to the persecutor, Give place, all of you, to me! Let me the first of you all fall down before His feet. Wonders in heaven: Yes! But on that day there will be two supreme wonders in heaven to every saved and sanctified and glorified sinner. There will be that wonder of wonders, Jesus Christ, and then there will be that other wonder of wonders, every saved and sanctified and glorified sinner himself. That is to say, Jesus Christ, and you and I. Amen.

VIII

I FILL UP THAT WHICH IS BEHIND OF THE SUFFERINGS OF CHRIST

I CAN well believe that some of you as often as you read this passage are led to say to yourselves, What can Paul possibly mean? For, how can he or any other mortal man, ever supplement anything to the sufferings of Christ? Did not Christ tread the winepress alone? And did He not exclaim with His latest breath, It is finished? Yes, most certainly so. Christ absolutely finished, and by Himself alone, all that awful work which His Father had laid on Him to do. And no man ever knew that better, or ever preached that better, than Paul did himself. What, then, can the Apostle possibly mean when he says that he, Paul, is continually filling up what Christ has left behind of His earthly sufferings? Yes, this is surely one of those things in the Epistles of his brother Paul that Peter found so hard to be understood. And, yet, with all our difficulty sometimes with Paul's depth and with his individuality, we continue to have the greatest confidence in what the chief of the Apostles says. So much so, that, whether we always find him to be easily understood or no, we continue to believe and to be sure that at bottom Paul has always the mind of Christ to convey to us.

Well, then, did you ever read anything, or did you ever hear anything preached, about that glorious relationship that subsists between Christ and the soul which is called in evangelical theology the Mystical Union? At any rate you all know what a union is if you do not as yet know what the Mystical Union is. It is a union, if not a mystical union, when a man and a woman are united and are made one in their marriage. Only, having written a beautiful chapter about a specially happy marriage that he had seen in Ephesus the Apostle winds up that beautiful chapter with these so suggestive words: "This is a great mystery; but I speak concerning Christ and the Church." There are marriage unions sometimes to be seen among ourselves such as Paul saw in the Church of Ephesus; marriage unions in which the husband and the wife are made one mind and one heart and one will and one wish in everything. You will sometimes have the happiness to see a marriage in which the wife has not only left her father's house and her father's name behind her, but almost her very self. Till she can say with her whole heart that she is scarcely any more her former self at all, she is so wholly swallowed up in her husband. Now, these are the very words, almost to a syllable, in which Paul so expatiates on his own mystical union with the Son of God. And it is out of the possession and the experience and the enjoyment of that mystical union of his that such otherwise impossible Scriptures as the text spring up and find their way into every one of Paul's Epistles. Indeed, this so absolute oneness of his with Christ is so ever-present and is so all-powerful with Paul that it fully accounts for the whole of his incomparable experiences and attainments and doctrines. This absolute oneness of Paul with the Son of God so accounts and so alone accounts for all that Paul possesses and performs and preaches, that unless his absolute oneness with the Son of God is always kept before our minds, it will be impossible for us to read Paul's sermons and his Epistles without being continually tempted to call out with Festus, that Paul is surely beside himself. It was the wonderful way that the mystical union opened Paul's mouth and lit up his countenance as he spoke his great apology that made King Agrippa confess that the prisoner had almost persuaded him to leave all his paganism and to become a Christian. Indeed, all up and down Paul's addresses and Epistles there abound passages that make the reader think that it is less Paul than very Christ Himself who there speaks and writes in and through Paul. Mystical union passages, of which this is perhaps the consummation and the crown, this: "I am crucified with Christ. Nevertheless I live: yet not I, but Christ liveth in me. And the life I live in the flesh I live by my faith in the Son of God, who loved me, and gave Himself for me." The Mystical Union can no further go than that—not in this life, at any rate. For this oneness of Paul's whole mind and heart and will with Christ is so real to him; it is so deep, it is so complete, and it is so perfect in every way to him; that even the apostolic doctrines of suretyship and substitution and imputation and atonement, all taken together, fall far short of that absolute identification of Paul's whole existence with Christ: that absolute identification which, in all Paul's so heavenly Epistles, includes and completes and explains and justifies all those so glorious Pauline doctrines that, all taken together, constitute Paul's supremely apostolic Gospel to the Church and to the world.

Neither Paul, nor any other mortal man, can ever come near Christ, nor can in any way whatever share with Christ in His sin-atoning sufferings for our salvation. Jesus Christ, by Himself alone, was delivered for our offences, and was raised again for our justification. But all these suretyship sufferings of His being for ever finished, when it comes to our personal and individual and experimental sanctification, then a real and an immense difficulty begins immediately to come into view. In your own spiritual and inward experiences, my believing brethren, and in the multitude of your anxious thoughts about yourselves, and about all your relations to Christ, and about all His relations to you, it will sometimes have staggered you and indeed greatly distressed you to think that your Great High Priest could never have had any of your experiences of inward sin and shame and suffering. With all His miraculous equipment, and with all His complete preparation for His office of Saviour, and with all His deep and true and *metrio-*

pathein sympathy with you, even so, He never had that awful experience of indwelling sin which makes you so wretched continually. No doubt, you will say to yourselves—no doubt He was in all points tempted outwardly as you are; but He was never tempted and tortured and killed inwardly as you are so incessantly. He was tempted and tortured and at last killed by men and devils; but He was never tempted and tortured and killed by His own devilish heart as you are every day. Now, it is just here, it is just at this so crucial point, that Paul comes in so wonderfully to fill up that which is left behind of the sufferings of Christ. Paul, that greatest of all the saints, comes in here with his awful soul-sufferings to be a forerunner and a pattern and an example to us of a kind of soul-suffering that it was simply not possible for Christ personally to experience. Christ once suffered for sin; and He so suffered for sin as to make an end of it to all His people in the most absolute and everlasting way. But, all the same, Christ did not suffer for His personal sinfulness as His holy apostle so agonizingly and so continually suffered, and as all true believers in their own appointed measure agonizingly and continually suffer. Christ, in Paul's awful words, was made sin for us: and, then, He was made a curse for us. But, with all that, He was never made, and He never made Himself actually a sinner. I do not forget that Luther in his evangelical fervour calls Christ the greatest sinner that ever was. And I know quite well what is in the great reformer's mind when he so passionately and so paradoxically speaks. But, made the greatest sinner that ever was by His suretyship and by the imputation of all our sins to Him, yet, with all that, Christ never tasted Luther's own maddening experience of a sinful heart. Christ tasted death indeed, but He never once tasted that inward death and hell: that personal sense of guilt and remorse and horror and self-hatred that Paul and Luther carried about with them all their regenerate life on earth. When on one disgraceful occasion He was surrounded and sickened with a scene of indescribable shame and pain in the temple, our Lord stooped down and wrote something mysterious on the floor of the temple. But at no time, neither in the temple nor anywhere else, did He ever stoop so far down as to write the seventh chapter of the Epistle to the Romans. Christ, at His lowest, left that last and uttermost suffering for Paul to fill up. And Paul filled that last suffering up every day he lived on earth, till you will all say with Thomas Goodwin that you will look to see Paul seated next to Christ Himself in heaven. Such were his sufferings, and all his other services, for Christ and for us his fellow-sinners his fellow-sufferers and his fellow-saints.

But while Christ was absolutely alone in His sufferings for Paul's justification and ours, Paul has by no means been alone in his sanctification sufferings for himself and for us. A great succession of God's truest saints have taken up Paul's inward cross and in the agony of it have followed the fore-running apostle in his long lifetime of soul-sanctification and soul-suffering. And foremost among them a great apostolical succession of evangelical preachers and pastors have so followed him. You are not preachers nor pastors, but it will do you no harm to be told how all true preachers and pastors are made ready to serve Christ and to serve you in the Gospel. Well, if you care to read it and understand it, you have the spiritual secret of their making in the text. Every single candidate for the evangelical ministry is made, in his measure, to fill up some secret soul-suffering that Christ has left behind Him as that candidate's preparation for the proper discharge of his future pulpit and pastoral work. The Apostle Paul never had a truer successor in the Gospel than Luther, and it was Luther's terrible soul-sufferings that made him the great reformer and great preacher and great pastor he was. " I was but a raw-headed monk," he tell us, " till Christ let the devil loose upon me. It was my experience of the tempter, and of my own heart under his assaults, that ever made me a preacher of Paul's Gospel. It was my own exceeding sinfulness of heart that ever more and more taught and compelled me to preach Christ alone in His blood and righteousness." " I was very fond of divinity books," said Thomas Halyburton to his divinity students standing around his deathbed. " And I got great good from my great divinity books. But it was what the Lord taught me of my own evil heart that was far more impressive and powerful with me than all my most spiritual books. Gentlemen," he said, as he raised himself up to speak to them for the last time, "be faithful and diligent and laborious night and day in the preparation of your sermons. But, above all else, scan well your own evil hearts, and then make use of what you discover there to enable you to scan and break other men's hearts, and then go on to introduce all such broken-hearted hearers to the true Physician. I preached much in my day to God's saints on Paul's sufferings under his great spiritual sanctification, and I do not repent that preaching now that I shall preach no more." So far that great Scottish scholar and great Covenanter saint, Thomas Halyburton, of St Andrews.

You will have heard many laments made in these last days about the distressing fewness of our divinity students. And many reasons have been given for that distressing deficiency. But the real reason is to be read in the text. It is because so few of our young men have entered for their own justification into Christ's sufferings for them, and then for their own sanctification into Paul's sufferings for them. In calling a young man to be a preacher and a pastor after His own heart, Christ comes to him and says to him, not—Are you able in these days conscientiously to subscribe and verbatim to your fathers' Calvinistic Confession of Faith? nor —Are you able to look forward to maintaining a family on the equal dividend? No. His only question to such a young man is this: Are you able to drink of My cup, and to be baptized with My baptism, and so to fill up what of My sufferings I have left behind for you so to fill up? And it is because so few of our young men understand their

Redeemer's words and respond to them that our college classes are so small, and that so many of our pulpits are so poorly filled. But there is every reason to believe that the low-water mark in that respect is past. The tide has already turned. And you may comfort your hearts with the assurance that the scholarly and doctrinal and evangelical and experimental pulpit, the Pauline and Puritan pulpit, has a great future before it in Scotland even as it has had such a great past in our highly favoured fatherland: highly favoured in its preaching above any other land under heaven.

But all that has been said about Paul's great soul-sufferings and Luther's and Halyburton's may not have come near your own case. All that you have ever read or heard preached about the awful sufferings that always accompany a supreme sanctification may not have seemed to you to come within a thousand miles of your own secret and incessant spiritual sufferings. Your own sinful heart is such, and your surrounding circumstances are such: you are so beset with such unparalleled temptations on all hands and at all times that with all the experimental literature you possess, scriptural and post-scriptural down to this day, your own experience is such that you have hitherto found no parallel to it, and have found no light cast upon it in all you have ever read or heard preached. I can well believe it. Indeed, I understand your sad and solitary case only too well. But do you not know, have you never read, that every true believer's life is as much a new and an unanticipated and an unparalleled spectacle and experience of human sinfulness; and, then, of divine grace, as if there had never been a Paul, or a Luther, or a Bunyan, or a Brea, or a Brodie, or an Edwards, or a Shepard, or a Halyburton, or a Boston, or a Chalmers before him? Human sinfulness is such an absolutely boundless universe of a thing: and, then, God's salvation is such a correspondingly absolutely boundless universe of a thing, that it takes every single one of that great multitude which God alone can number to exhibit all the breadth, and length, and depth and height, and all the unspeakable malignity and persistency of sin; and, then, over against all that, to exhibit all the much more abounding grace of God. And all the personal sufferings of the Man of Sorrows Himself both in His own body and in His own soul; and all His mystical sufferings in the bodies and souls of all His members is all needed, every agonizing pang of it, in order to display all the wisdom, and all the power, and all the grace, and all the glory of God in the Gospel. And your personal and individual share in all that sin and in all that suffering and in all that grace and in all that glory may be as real and as deep as was the share of the great Apostle himself. For, if you suffer with Christ in your sanctification as Paul suffered with Him, then you shall also reign with Christ in glory as Paul now reigns. Aye, as much so as if you had written the seventh of the Romans with your own hand and in your own heart's blood.

On the Mystical Union—if you have spiritual understanding and spiritual enterprise enough—

read Walter Marshall's masterpiece, published by Messrs Nisbet at a shilling.[1] A small book, but a true masterpiece—especially " The Third Direction."

[1] "The book you mention lies now upon my table. Marshall is an old acquaintance of mine. I think him one of the best writers, and the most spiritual expositor of Scripture I have ever read."—WILLIAM COWPER'S *Twenty-first Letter*.

IX

PAUL MADE A SPECTACLE: GREEK AND MARGIN—A THEATRE

"I AM a man," said an ancient moralist, "and nothing that in any way concerns mankind is without its interest to me." Now the Apostle Paul repeated that and greatly improved upon that in all his Epistles. And that rich humanity of his, that great breadth of mind of his, and that great depth and tenderness of heart of his, all that is revealed to us in every Epistle of his, and all that fully accounts for his so great liking for the great Greek classics. It is a very remarkable and a very significant fact that the Apostle goes out of his way again and again, as some might think, in order to make use of choice and telling quotations from some great Greek authors. As Newman says in a splendid sermon, Paul greatly yearned over our poor fallen human nature, and that with a passionate pity and a passionate love, even as his Master did. Now the dramatic literature of the great Greek tragedians was the best expression and the best exhibition of pagan human nature in the Apostle's day. And this is how we are able to account for his so familiar acquaintance with the great Greek dramatists. And this is how we are able to account also for his so frequent references to the spectacular exhibitions of the Greek and Latin stage.

In his fine preface to "Samson Agonistes," Milton says that tragedy, as it was anciently composed, hath been ever held to be the gravest, the moralest, and the most profitable of all other poems. Therefore, says Milton, it is said by Aristotle to be of great power to cleanse and to heal the soul of the spectator. And it was this that so drew the noble mind of John Milton first to the study, and then to the imitation, of the great Greek tragedians. And it was the same thing in the great Greek tragedians that would lead a man of Paul's greatness of mind and holiness of heart to read and to see and to hear as often as he had fit opportunity such masterpieces as Æschylus and Sophocles put upon the solemnising stage of Athens and Corinth and Colosse. And, that being so, I can hear some intellectual and spiritual pupil of the Apostle asking him if his people had anything in Jerusalem or in Samaria like the great Greek masterpieces, such as the Agamemnon, or the Œdipus, or the Prometheus. No, Paul would reply. No. Our Hebrew forefathers did not favour the stage. Not that they did not have abundance of the most tragical materials both in their family life and in their national history. The fact is, Paul would affably reply, in our ancient Hebrew books we have the greatest tragedies that this world has ever seen. To begin with, we have what is known in Israel as the unspeakably awful tragedy

of Adam and Eve, which is the fountainhead and
the true original of all the soul-cleansing tragedies
that have ever taken place on the face of the earth.
Yes, we have Adam and Eve, and we have Cain and
Abel, and we have Noah and his vineyard, and we
have Sarah and Hagar her handmaid, and we have
Abraham and his son Isaac, and we have Jacob
and Esau, and we have Joseph and his brethren,
and we have Samson and Delilah, and we have Job,
a tragedy dramatically written out and ready indeed
to our hand, and we have David and the matter of
Uriah.

> And if I would delight my private hours
> With music or with poem, where so soon
> As in our native language can I find
> That solace ?   All our law and story strew'd
> With hymns, our psalms with artful terms inscribed,
> Our Hebrew songs and harps, in Babylon
> That pleased so well our victors' ears, declare
> That rather Greece from us these arts deriv'd.
> Par. Reg., iv. 331-8.

Yes, were all our Hebrew tragedies to be
put upon the stage I am quite sure that neither
Athens nor Rome ever saw such soul-cleansing and
such soul-healing spectacles. So Paul would compare and contrast his Old Testament histories with
the great classics of the Greek and Latin world.
" But the whole of human history," says the Abbot
of Buckfast, " so full of the cruellest tragedies,
has no tragedy like the tragedy of Christ. For
the hope for which St Paul lived became its curse
through that awful misunderstanding which the
Gospel calls blindness of heart. St Paul has char-

acterised the terrible irony of these things with the genius of a Sophocles. But nothing could show more clearly the bitterness of that tragedy than St Luke's picture of Christ weeping over Jerusalem."

'Now,' writes Paul to the Church of God at Corinth, 'all these things, brethren, I have in a figure transferred to myself and to Apollos for your sakes. For I think that God hath set forth us apostles, as it were, appointed to death; we are made a spectacle indeed, as in a theatre, unto the world, and to angels, and to men. That is to say, as the great Greek spectacles of virtue and of vice; of how his sin always finds the sinner out, and of how true and timeous repentance always propitiates and placates the offended gods of Olympus; as all these things are put upon your Greek stage, so you may see in me and in Apollos how the only true God makes His apostles a spectacle of suffering and of salvation, to be seen of the world, and of angels, and of men.' Now, we do not know much about Apollos beyond the interesting information that he was a Jew of Alexandria, an eloquent man, and mighty in the Scriptures, and that he watered with great success where Paul had previously planted. We know nothing of Apollos beyond that; and as to the tragedies of his life, to which Paul here refers, we are left in complete ignorance of them. But Paul himself and his so tragical and so spectacular life fills the half of our New Testament. In fact, take Paul first and last; take him in all the events and in all the experiences of his outward life; and then take him in all the unparalleled experiences and sufferings and attainments of his inward life, and he thus affords us by far the most instructive and the most impressive spectacle of God's ways with men that ever was put upon the stage of human life; the most instructive and the most impressive spectacle by far, next to the unapproachable spectacle of our Lord Himself. In his apprentice days in Tarsus; in his student days in Jerusalem; in his persecuting days in Jerusalem, those sinful days that left such a running sore in his heart to the end of his life; in his conversion days and nights in Damascus; in his so fruitful three years in Arabia, and in all his subsequent years of preaching and of writing and of an unparalleled sanctification—in all that Paul is the most complete and perfect spectacle that God ever put upon the Hebrew or the Christian stage. As Paul again and again says himself, he was a matchless spectacle and pattern of sin and of salvation, of the work of Christ for him, and of the work of the Holy Spirit within him; a spectacle and a pattern that far eclipses, not only the best spectacles of the Greek stage, but far eclipses, for divine instruction and for divine impression, the best examples of the Old Testament itself, rich as so many of those examples are in what is fitted to cleanse the soul from sense and sin. A great man has said that to him the *Summa* of St Thomas was a greater epic than Homer's Odyssey; and much more may that be said of the personal Epistles of St Paul. The Book of the Acts and the whole of Paul's own thirteen Epistles are as full as they can hold of the scenes and the *dramatis personæ*, divine and human, that everywhere people Paul's so spectacular life. But passing by his so spectacular outward life, there is one quite classical passage in which he concentrates our whole attention on his exceeding sinfulness and ill desert; and, then, on the still more exceeding grace of God. The passage is deservedly classical: "According to the glorious Gospel of the Blessed God, which was committed to my trust. And I thank Jesus Christ our Lord, who hath enabled me, for that He counted me faithful, putting me into the ministry; who was before a blasphemer, and a persecutor, and injurious; but I obtained mercy, because I did it in unbelief. This is a faithful saying, and worthy of all acceptation, that Christ Jesus came into the world to save sinners, of whom I am chief. Howbeit, for this cause I obtained mercy, that in me first Jesus Christ might show forth all long-suffering, for a pattern to them which should hereafter believe in Him to life everlasting." In his own eyes Paul always eclipses by far every other sinner in his great sinfulness. And thus it is that he steps out upon this scriptural stage and proclaims himself to be the most perfect pattern and spectacle anywhere to be seen of the grace of God and of the salvation that is always to be found in Jesus Christ.

There is a famous ancient saying to the effect that a good man struggling against a great adversity is a spectacle altogether worthy of the gods themselves looking down upon with sympathy and with approval and with help. And so it is. Only, the greatest and best of the ancient tragedians did not yet know the greatest by far of all human adversities, and, consequently, they could not put it upon their pagan stage. The law of a spiritual and an evangelical holiness had not as yet entered the mind or the imagination of Æschylus or Sophocles. And, that being the case, they could not possibly portray experimentally and dramatically the unceasing agony of a truly spiritual man under the supreme adversity of his own indwelling and inexpugnable sinfulness. In their great civility the magistrates of Athens were wont to supply the poorest of the people with free passes into the theatre when some of the great tragedies of adversity were put upon the stage. To what extent and to what result the common people availed themselves of their great opportunities and great privileges I do not know. Neither can I be quite sure how many of you avail yourselves of your great opportunities of salvation and sanctification when Paul's spiritual adversities, his spiritual conflicts, and his spiritual conquests are made a spectacle to the world, and to angels, and to men, in his great experimental and autobiographical Epistles. But Paul could always count on one Spectator, whose presence and whose understanding and whose sympathy he could always rely upon, especially in his greatest adversities. All Paul's more than Prometheus-agony of soul; all his all but Gethsemane and Calvary-agony of soul, was always enacted and displayed under the sleepless eye of his God and Saviour Jesus Christ. Paul had the most absolute assurance that his Risen Lord was always near him when he was again undergoing the pain and the shame and the Œdipus-like horror and the whole unspeakable wretchedness of his cruel bondage to his remaining sinfulness; a cruel bondage that he both loathed and hated like hell. The Caucasian rock to which Prometheus was chained with clamps of iron was a bed of roses compared with that body of sin and death with which Paul had to agonize all his days on earth. But in all that unspeakable wretchedness of his he had always One Spectator whose simple presence at the tragical spectacle always made Paul endure it and come out of it more than a conqueror.

Now, my brethren, you do not need to go to the Prometheus of Æschylus, nor to the Œdipus of Sophocles, nor to the Epistles of Paul to see a spectacle quite sufficient to cleanse your souls by the terror of the Lord, and still more by His soul-redeeming grace. For, within these four commonplace-looking walls this Sabbath morning there are being displayed spectacles of human hearts and lives down into which God Himself is even now looking, and for the everlasting issues of which He is continually watching. Yes, and if we may trust the Scriptures on this great matter, not God only, but He shares His interest and His anxiety with His holy angels. We are again and again assured that those blessed beings were admitted to feast their holy hearts on Paul and on his fellow-apostles when they were being made a spectacle of God and of His grace and truth. And it is not at all past belief that the principalities and powers who desire to look into the things of your salvation may have free seats allotted them from which they look down from time to time to see how you perform your part on the great occasions, tragical and other, that come to you in your personal and in your family life, in your private and in your public life. And thus, you may be well assured, there are high days in heaven when there is a new joy in heaven over the entrances and the issues of personal and domestic tragedies that down here seem to you but sent to break your heart. For where they sit those heavenly spectators collect and record from a long observation that all things—the darkest things, the cruellest things, the most tragical things—always in the long event turn out for the greatest good to them who are rightly exercised by these tragical things. Dante greatly startles us at first sight when he entitles his terrible book a comedy. But when we read on we come to see that he so names his great poem because, tragically as it opens and proceeds, yet it ends at last in a peace and in a joy and in a rapture of blessedness that even his incomparable pen is quite unable to describe. Yes, be you all absolutely sure of this, that to God's eyes, and to the eyes of His ministering spirits, within these everyday walls there are spectacles being seen, sometimes as tragical, and sometimes as gracious and as eventually blessed, as those clear and holy eyes of heaven have ever seen. For Adam and his awful fall are being seen here this day. Cain also, and his envy and his hatred and his murder of his brother. Noah also is here with all the tragedy and all the entailed curse of his appetite for wine—preacher of righteousness to other people as he was and is. Sarah also and all her inhuman treatment of Hagar is here. And Jacob also with his evil eye on his brother's birthright is here; and sitting beside him Esau, who has sold his birthright for far less than a mess of pottage. Abraham also is here, and Joseph, and Moses, and Job, and David, both in his great sin and in his great repentance. But who are not here as spectacles of temptations, and of falls, and of the wages of sin; and, again, of faith, and repentance, and prayer, and patience, and cup-drinking, and cross-bearing, and of a furnace of sanctification seven times heated? All the tragedies possible in the pagan dispensation were but the entertainment and amusement of a Greek holiday, compared with the tragedies, impossible to be escaped, under the Christian dispensation when its terrible discipline once really enters the but partially regenerate Christian heart. "God and I," said John Howe, "are spectacle enough for one another, when I am placed on the stage of my so tragical sanctification." "They are theatre enough to one another," said even Seneca. And Father Faber somewhere says on this same subject that every truly spiritual man's life is a special spectacle to himself both of the severity and the goodness of God.

But, on the other hand, and all the time, some of you sitting here and looking so innocent may be a spectacle to God and to His holy angels, not of faith like Abraham, nor of meekness like Moses, nor of the blessedness of forgiveness like David, nor of cross-bearing like Christ, nor of a great spiritual sanctification like Paul. But, on the other hand, you may be a spectacle of the cause of all these things in other people; in some one, it may be, in your own family, and in the same unhappy house with you. You may be to God a spectacle of a hard heart, of cruel conduct, of the most abominable selfishness, and of an utter indifference to the sin and the suffering you are causing every day to those who are ill fated to live near you. You may be a delightful spectacle to the devil himself because you are doing his diabolical work for him in a place where, without you, he could not do it; and in a way he could not, without you, do it. And all the cross-bearing, and all the patience, and all the endurance, and all the sin also that you are causing to other people, may be being set down to be settled with you when the books are opened at the great day of righteous retribution. You should look to it. You should look at yourself as God looks at you. You should look at yourself as your victim looks at you. You should ask yourself how your life looks and tastes to your father, or to your mother, or to your sister, or to your brother, or to anyone else whose life you are making a spectacle of suffering of any kind. Ask your own conscience, and you will not be left in any doubt about how you look in the eyes of those whose lives are being made a tragedy by you. God is slow to anger, as your long forborne life sufficiently proves. But He can be angry. And, then, there is a spectacle indeed! You should see to it, and that before it is too late.

X

PAUL'S APOSTOLICAL PHILOSOPHY

WHEN the Apostle warns his readers to beware lest any man should spoil them through philosophy he is not thinking about Greek philosophy nor about German philosophy nor about French philosophy nor about our own so famous Scottish philosophy. He is not referring to Socrates nor to Descartes nor to Kant nor to Locke nor to Reid nor to Sir William Hamilton. Paul is speaking home to his own day and to a philosophy of his own day falsely so-called. He is not denouncing nor belittling any really genuine philosophy, ancient or modern; no, not for a moment. For a genuine philosophy is a right noble thing, even as it bears a right noble name. And philosophy got its right noble name in this right noble way. Some hundreds of years before the advent of our Lord there lived in Greece a truly great and a truly good man named Pythagoras. The seven sages of Greece lived long before his day and he was one of their true successors. On being asked on one occasion if he would allow his disciples to add his name as the eighth of the shining roll he said No, certainly not. For he said that he was by no means a wise man; he was at his best only a lover of wisdom and a somewhat diligent student thereof. Well, then, said his admiring scholars, we will call you a *philosopher*, coining a new Greek word to describe their wise and modest master. And thus it arose and came about that any man of an exceptionally able, exceptionally thoughtful, and exceptionally penetrating mind in Greece and in Rome was called a philosopher; that is to say, a lover of wisdom. " Wherefore it is to be observed," says Dante, " that a true philosopher does not bear a name of pride, and pretension, and arrogance; but a name of meekness, and of humility, and of all childlike teachableness."

" Philosophy," says our best Edinburgh text-book, " is a rational explanation of all existing things. Philosophy is the ultimate explanation of how and why such and such things exist. Thinking men are compelled to seek into the innermost nature of things: how they came into existence, and why. As also, to try to gather up into a unity the multitudes of things that exist, and to reduce their endless variety to law and order and rule. And it is when a man is so employed that he is said to be prosecuting philosophy." And the father of English philosophy has this in his Advancement of Learning: " The contemplations of men do either penetrate unto God, or they are circumferred to nature, or they are reverted upon men themselves. Out of which several inquiries there do arise these three philosophies: first, Divine Philosophy; second, Natural Philosophy; and third, the Philosophy of Humanity." So far Bacon himself.

Now, from all that, it will be seen at once how great a thing a true philosophy is; how great, how high, and how noble a thing it is. But, then, its very greatness, its very height and depth and nobility are all so great that the greatest and the best philosophers have always been the first to confess that after they had done their best, the true and the full and the final interpretation of things, both divine and human, had completely baffled them. Take that which is nearest us: take our human existence itself, and what an utterly insoluble problem it has been to the ablest and the best philosophy in all ages and in all lands. How did this world of ours come into existence? And at what time? But the previous question of philosophy is this, What is time itself? And what was before time, and what will be after it? And what is man himself, and how came he to be what he is? What is the purpose, the end, and the final cause of man's existence? What is his chief good, and what is his chief evil? And how is he to escape all his evil and to attain to all his good? To think seriously about such questions as these,—even to attempt to state such questions as these—that is already the beginning of a true philosophy. And that shows us how wise a man Pythagoras was, and how impossible it is for any mortal man to be a real, a true, a successful, and a final philosopher. The most and the best that any mortal man can do in the face of such problems as these is to live, and to think, and to study in humility, and in awe, and in faith, and in love, and in hope, as all the wisest men of the pagan dispensation did, with Pythagoras and Socrates and Plato at their head. "Forbid," said Dr Chalmers, "that any philosophy should ever seduce me from the simplicity that is in Christ. I have often been comforted by that passage where the Apostle adverts to the oppositions of science 'falsely so-called.' It is false science only that he abjures, and this is tantamount to the recognition of true science."

But to return to our text-book: "Philosophy supplies the most rational explanation of existing things. It gives the ultimate explanation of our own existence and of all the conditions and circumstances of our own existence." Just so. And that is exactly what our present philosopher, the Apostle Paul, does in every Epistle of his. Look around you, he says to all his readers. Look abroad at the whole of humanity: Jew and Greek; learned and unlearned; wise and simple; and, then, look within at the nature and the condition of your own heart. And, when you have done all that, I will give you the only rational philosophy of all that. And, then, into the hands of every truly prepared, serious-minded, and teachable reader, the Apostle places his own divinely inspired Epistles. Sir Alexander Grant says that Aristotle but codified Plato. And it is but the intelligent and evangelical truth to say that in all his Epistles Paul but codified Christ. As an Egyptian father of the desert has it, Matthew and Mark and Luke and John supplied

F

the wool indeed, but it was Paul who span the wool and wove and cut and fitted on the garment. As thus: " Where is the wise? Where is the scribe? Where is the disputer of this world? Hath not God made foolish the wisdom of this world? For, after that, in the wisdom of God, the world by wisdom knew not God, it pleased God by the foolishness of preaching Christ crucified to save them that believe." And, again, "that your hearts may be comforted, being knit together in love, and unto all riches of the full assurance of understanding: to the acknowledgment of the mystery of God, and of the Father, and of Christ, in whom are hid all the treasures of wisdom and knowledge. Beware, therefore, lest any man spoil you through his false philosophy and not after Christ. For in Him dwelleth all the fulness of the Godhead bodily. For by Him were all things created that are in heaven, and that are on earth: all things were created by Him and for Him, and by Him all things consist. For it pleased the Father that in Him should all fulness dwell; and having made peace by the blood of His cross to reconcile all things to Himself. And you, that were sometime alienated and enemies in your mind by wicked works, yet now hath He reconciled to present you holy, and unreproveable, and unblameable in His sight." Now, what say you to that for a rational, a philosophical, an ultimate, and a final explanation of yourselves, and of all created and fallen and restored men and things? What say you to that, and to all like that in Paul, as a reduction of all things around you and within you to a unity of law and order and heavenly harmony? Whatever you may feel and say, I feel sure that Paul's Gospel would have carried Plato's fine mind captive. For sure I am the apostolical and evangelical philosophy is the exact "raft" that Plato so longed to see launched on the tempestuous seas of life and thought amid which he waded out so deeply in his pre-Christian day. O the depth, he would have exclaimed, both of the wisdom and the knowledge of God! For who hath known the mind of the Lord? Or who hath been His counsellor? For of Him, and through Him, and to Him are all things, to whom be glory for ever. Amen. So the author of the Dialogues would have subscribed to the author of the Epistles: and, indeed, is now so subscribing.

The fulness and the perfection of the philosophical temper of mind was first exhibited in the New Testament believer. That is Dr Newman's argument in a perfect gem of a University sermon. And in his own exquisite way Newman argues out that thesis in a manner that must have made a lifelong impression on his Oxford audience. In that fascinating style which is all his own the commanding preacher proves that the intellectual temper and the moral and spiritual character that the Gospel alone creates and fosters is the very same mental and moral character that both the best science and the best philosophy demand in their best students. The temper and the character that is of a deeply felt and a constantly admitted ignorance, and of a sincere and a single-minded love of truth; the intellectual and spiritual temper of humility of mind, and modesty, and reverence, and patience, and teachableness, and hopefulness, and true piety. Now, if that is so—and, past all question, that is so—then lift up your heads and cheer your hearts all you who are of a humble mind and a devout and gracious temper. For the Apostle has you in his eye when he says to you: " Ye see your calling, brethren, how that not many wise men after the flesh, not many mighty, not many noble are called." Now, you would laugh at yourselves if any man were to call you wise, or mighty, or noble. And far more if any man were to call you wiser and better than the wise and noble of this world. You would say to us not to mock you and befool you if we were ever to call you of a philosophical mind and character, unlearned and ignorant men like you. But neither the Apostle nor the Oxford preacher is mocking nor befooling you. Far, far from that. The Apostle is certain that he has the mind of Christ Himself concerning you when he enlists and enrols you as a true scholar in His apostolical and evangelical, aye, and even his philosophical school. And it is with the most perfect confidence in your lowly mind and in your humble heart and in your consequently enlightened understanding, that he puts into your hands his so profound and so philosophical Epistles. All the same, and after all such things are said, you will still shrink back from the name of a philosopher or a theologian or a saint. But so did Pythagoras, and so did Paul himself. " Not that I have attained," he deprecated, " either am already perfect, but I follow after, and I press toward the mark and toward the prize."

How proud of your son you would be if it was announced in the newspapers that he had attained to a first-class certificate in philosophy! How your heart would swell over him and over his high intellectual distinction! But reflect on this. Even if your lowly-born son has to spend all his days in a carpenter's or in a tent-maker's workshop, he is not, because of that, debarred from the pursuit and the attainment of the highest and the best philosophy. "'From a child," wrote the greatest of apostles and philosophers to the son of Eunice, "thou hast known the Holy Scriptures, which are able to make thee wise unto salvation: that the man of God may be perfect, thoroughly furnished to all good works." And all men, young and old, learned and unlearned, carpenter and tentmaker; all men who have the Holy Scriptures in their hands have in them the true wisdom: the true apostolical and evangelical philosophy. And they all have nature also if, as Bacon has it, their thoughts are sufficiently circumferred to nature and to the God of nature. I remember to this day a philosophical and a theological and a truly religious lesson I got when I was a child of nine or ten years old. A flower-show was being held in his native town and Dr Burns Thomson, of the Cowgate Dispensary, had come north to open the show. I was standing at his feet looking up reverently at the great man, when, toward the end of his opening speech, he waved his hand over the wide display of beautiful flowers and fruits and quoting Cowper said: "But the best of it all is this, that our Heavenly Father made them all." I have never forgot that proclamation of his that day. Indeed, to this day I never enter a summer garden or a conservatory or a flower-show that my swelling heart does not remind me that my Heavenly Father's power and wisdom and beauty and love are all spread out before me. And, then, ever since I learned my Christological Philosophy from Athanasius and Newman and Dorner and Rainy at the New College, I have been enabled to enlarge and to enrich Cowper's and Dr Burns Thomson's noble words, and to say with the Apostle, " In whom we have redemption through His blood, even the forgiveness of sins. And by Him were all things created that are in heaven and that are on earth; all things were created by Him and for Him: and by Him all things consist." Whether or no then your son is a philosophical student, conventionally so called, all the same he has God, and he has Jesus Christ, and he has nature, and he has himself, and all these are as open to his study as they are to the most privileged student in all the University. Teach your son then from his earliest days to see and to say that his Heavenly Father made all created things, and that He made them all by and through and for His well-beloved Son Jesus Christ your Saviour and your son's Saviour. Bequeath to him when you die, not silver and gold, but the true riches of wisdom and knowledge, so that he shall all his days on earth sing with David concerning his God and Father, and say :—

Who made the earth and heavens high,
    Who made the swelling deep,
And all that is within the same ;
    Who truth doth ever keep.
He counts the number of the stars,
    He names them every one ;
Great is our Lord, and of great power,
    His wisdom search can none.

And to sing with Solomon and with William Cowper this gloriously philosophical and sapiential song :—

Ere God had built the mountains,
    Or raised the fruitful hills,
Before He filled the fountains
    That feed the running rills ;
In Me, from everlasting,
    The wonderful I Am
Found pleasures never wasting,
    And WISDOM is My Name.

When, like a tent to dwell in,
    He spread the skies abroad,
And swathed about the swelling
    Of ocean's mighty flood ;
He wrought by weight and measure,
    And I was with Him then ;
Myself the Father's pleasure,
    And mine the sons of men.

Thus WISDOM'S words discover
    Thy glory and Thy grace,
Thou Everlasting Lover
    Of our unworthy race !
Thy gracious eye surveyed us,
    Ere stars were seen above ;
In wisdom Thou hast made us,
    And died for us in love.

And, couldst Thou be delighted
   With creatures such as we,
Who, when we saw Thee, slighted,
   And nailed Thee to a tree ?
Unfathomable wonder
   And mystery divine !
The voice that speaks in thunder
   Says, Sinner, I am thine !

XI

PAUL'S HYPERBOLES

HYPERBOLE, a Greek word which, taken literally, is simply "a throwing beyond," soon came to mean something above and beyond the ordinary rule: something carried to a certain excess: something carried to a certain exaggeration. And, now, in English literature an hyperbole is a familiar figure of speech employed to give expression to some strong emotion in the speaker's mind; while, all the time, the speaker's hyperbolical words are not intended, nor are expected, to be taken literally and severely. As Longinus says in his classical treatise on *The Sublime*, "The best hyperboles are those which are not noticed as hyperboles at all, being uttered in an outburst of strong feeling, and in harmony with a certain grandeur in the crisis described." Now, as was to be expected, the Holy Scriptures are full of such hyperboles. As, for instance, when the LORD said to Abraham, "I will make thy seed as the dust of the earth; so that if a man can number the dust of the earth, then shall thy seed also be numbered." Again, there is hyperbole upon hyperbole in the report of the spies: "The

Canaanites are greater and taller than we; their cities are walled up to heaven; there also we saw the sons of Anak, and we were in our own sight as grasshoppers, and so were we in their sight." Again: David's lament over Saul and Jonathan has this fine hyperbole: " They were lovely and sweet in their lives, and in their death they were not divided: they were swifter than eagles, they were stronger than lions. O my brother Jonathan, thy love to me was wonderful, passing the love of women." Then there is David's evangelical hyperbole in the fifty-first Psalm: " I shall be whiter than the snow." But Homer had that hyperbole long before David; only, Homer is singing of snow-white horses, whereas David is singing of snow-white saints. An ancient commentator's remark on Homer is this, that every true hyperbole transcends the possible, for there could be nothing whiter than snow. And there is John's noble hyperbole concerning the things that his Master said and did: " The which, if they should be written every one, I suppose that even the world itself could not contain the books that should be written." Nor did our Lord Himself despise the aid of the hyperbole in His preaching, as when He spoke of a camel going through the eye of a needle, and faith as a grain of mustard seed, and of the stones in the streets of Jerusalem crying out Hosanna to welcome His coming for their salvation. All of which are so many excellent illustrations of Longinus' principle that the excellence of an hyperbole lies in this, that it is not thought of as an hyperbole, but is taken as far truer than the literal truth itself.

But it is with Paul's apostolical hyperboles that we have here to do. Now, Paul is the most hyperbolical of all writers, and that is so because he writes on the most hyperbolical of all subjects. That is to say, he writes on sin and on grace, on God's love and on God's power, and on all that as experienced and preached by himself. And, then, as regards Paul's peculiar style in the whole of his writings, it is an old rule of interpretation that Paul alone is his own true interpreter. That is to say, there is no other possible interpreter of Paul but Paul himself. And, now, with that warning we are able to enter on some of Paul's great hyperboles. And, first, and as the foundation of them all, take what he says about sin. Sin, says Goodwin, in Paul's experience of it, and in his apostolic doctrine of it, is such an evil thing that it cannot have a worse epithet given to it, than just to call it sin. And thus it is that when the Apostle would speak his very worst of sin, and would wind up his words to their very highest—*usque ad hyperbolem*—he calls sin by its own supremely evil name, sinful sin. Sin, he says again, is above all measure sinful. The sinfulness of sin hath an hyperbole in it; man's utmost wit cannot reach up to all the sinfulness of sin. And, again, he calls original sin sinning sin. And this sinning sin it was, his own indwelling sin it was, that so continually humbled and broke the Apostle's heart all his days. In his holy eye, all his days, the unspeakable sinfulness of his heart was not only essential and pure sin: it was also the alone mother and the sure source of all his other sin. John Bunyan, one of Paul's best interpreters, has this hyperbolical song concerning sin :——

> Sin is the living worm, the lasting fire;
> Hell soon would lose its flames could sin expire.
> Better sinless in hell, than to be where
> Heaven is, and to be found a sinner there.
> One sinless with infernals might do well,
> But sin would make of heaven a very hell.
>   Look to thyself then, keep it out of door,
>   Lest it get in and never leave thee more.

And that great hyperbole concerning sin leads Paul on to a still greater hyperbole concerning grace. The only thing in the whole universe that is more hyperbolical than Paul's sinfulness is the exceeding grace of God toward Paul. The law entered Paul that the offence might become like the waves of the sea : but when his sin was as the waves of the sea, the grace of God, like an infinitely vaster sea, poured all its waves over Paul and over all Paul's sin, so that as his sin had reigned unto death in Paul, even so, grace now reigned through Christ's blood and righteousness to everlasting life in Paul. The grace of God was exceeding abundant toward Paul. The very windows of heaven opened and remained open over Paul, till from being the greatest vessel of wrath in all the world, he became the greatest vessel of saving grace in all the world. And here Goodwin strikes in with this : All the time, the hyperbole of grace, the exceeding riches of grace, comes in through the sin-atoning blood of Christ : and thus, the grace of God becomes dyed in the blood of Christ. And, as David said, What can Thy servant say more? Indeed, there is but this more to be said, that the riches of God's grace are so hyperbolical that eternity will not fully reveal, far less exhaust them. The wages of sin is death, but the gift of God is eternal life through Jesus Christ our Lord. And, then, when Paul is led back by the Holy Ghost to the great love of God out of which all God's grace always springs, he has no other word for that love but the word the Holy Ghost is always giving him; it is a love absolutely surpassing and hyperbolical. The Apostle makes it his excuse for not writing adequately about God's love, because it passeth his knowledge. That is to say, it cannot be written about as if it were a thing fully known to him who preaches and writes about it. The most spiritual mind even cannot fully comprehend it: the renewed and loving heart can alone taste the sweetness and the savour of the love of God. Says Goodwin: As the seat and source of God's love is God's own heart: so the human vessel into which the Holy Ghost pours that love is the loving heart of the true saint. And the eternity of that love, the sovereignty of it, the freeness of it, the omnipotence of it, the inexhaustibleness of it, and the exquisite intimacy and the indescribable sweetness of it—all that makes Paul's writing about it to be set forth in his only possible words; the words which the Holy Ghost teaches him; the words of a rapturous hyperbole; a rapturous hyperbole of which all his Epistles are full.

But there is nothing to which Paul returns so often and with such strength of language as to the power of God; His power that is working out Paul's salvation. And the reason of that so frequent return to God's power is Paul's deep sense of the absolutely divine power that will all be needed to the working out of his own so difficult salvation. Speaking after the manner of men, we may truly love some one, but we may not be able to perform for him what our love would prompt us to do. But not so God. As Dante says, with God love and power are one. And says Goodwin: Paul calleth it not only power, but greatness of power. And not content with that he calls it hyperbolical power: it is exceeding, superexcellent, sublime, overcoming, triumphing power. Almighty God is able to do exceeding abundantly above all we can ask or think. If God be for us, who can be against us? For His is the kingdom, and the power, and the glory.

> Art thou afraid His power shall fail
>   When comes thy evil day?
> And can an all-creating arm
>   Grow weary or decay?
> Let troubles rise, and terrors frown,
>   And days of darkness fall;
> Through Him all danger we'll defy,
>   And more than conquer all.

And, then, as to the heavenly glory, says Goodwin, I will name but one place and so leave it: the place is this: For our light affliction, which is but for a moment, worketh for us a far more exceeding and eternal weight of glory. That word there which is translated "far more exceeding" is in the original hyperbole upon hyperbole, that is, one hyperbole will not suffice to express it. Saith the Apostle, express heaven by hyperboles, and when you have done, still tumble one hyperbole upon another, and all that will not express it. I remember when he speaks of sin, he says that it is above measure sinful: the sinfulness of it hath an hyperbole in it: the wit of man cannot reach unto it. And, now, when he comes to speak of heaven, it has one hyperbole upon another: it is an exceeding and an hyperbolical glory and blessedness.

And, now, I will wind up all that with one other most appropriate hyperbole of the Apostle: his hyperbole about prayer. Pray without ceasing, he says. Yes, since we all sin without ceasing, he says, let us repent and pray without ceasing. Let us repent and pray without ceasing for all our past sins, and for all our present sinfulness; and then let us still pray without ceasing for a clean heart against all further sinfulness. Let us pray, he says, and without ceasing, till time and sin together cease. I wonder if the Thessalonians, to whom Paul wrote that happy hyperbole, understood it and did it. I would like to have had a talk with any one of them who understood it and did it. But since all who understood it and did it have now for long been home in the hyperbolical glory, let us who remain often speak together and encourage one another in the life of unceasing prayer. And if we have no unceasing neighbours, we have an abundance of unceasing authors from Paul down to

Goodwin, and from Goodwin down to our own day. Sell your bed, said unceasing Coleridge, and buy the best book on prayer.

"Sun, moon, and stars, and passages of Shakespeare," says Keats in a great hyperbole about the greatest of poets. And, now, in closing, I will borrow that great hyperbole, will improve upon it, will make it both legitimate and appropriate and true, and will say, Sun, moon, and stars, and passages of Paul. Such passages of Paul as all the above, and such hyperbolical passages as fill to overflowing all the great Epistles of the great Apostle.

XII

VERBA IN RES

"VERBA in res, as that philosopher said when he was converted." That is to say, all that philosopher's hitherto idle words became the greatest of realities to him when he was converted. Before his conversion that philosopher had made use on occasion of not a few scriptural and spiritual words; but, all the time, they were but so many idle words to him. Before his conversion there were no realities corresponding to the idle words that he so frequently employed. Before his conversion he would frequently read and write and speak and hear spoken these four great words: God, and God's Son, and sin, and salvation. But these greatest of all words made no impression on his mind and awoke no emotion in his heart. No awful and overwhelming reality ever arose in his imagination or in his conscience at the mention of His dread Name with whom he would one day have to do. And if you had said to him that, for your part, every time you read or heard read that awfulest of words to you, sin, a cold shudder came over you, he would have said to you that you were beside yourself and that you should lose no time in taking a course of polite literature or a class of mind-emancipating philosophy. Whereas both Bishop Butler and Cardinal Newman, two of the greatest philosophers and greatest men of letters in the English language, have arraigned literature, and even philosophy, as tending, even at their very best, to produce in their followers an idle, an unreal, and indeed an immoral use of words. "Literature," says the author of the Grammar of Assent, "is in its essence an unreal thing, for it is an exhibition of thought disjoined from action: it is an exhibition of words disjoined from realities."

But this was the immediate result of our philosopher's conversion that it at once and for ever conjoined all his great words with their own great realities. I come from the Town of Stupidity, says old Mr Honest when he is giving us an account of his conversion. My native town, he confesses to us, lies four degrees further away from the sun than even the City of Destruction itself. And thus it is that every man in our town, both learned man and simpleton, is a perfect mountain of ice both in his intellects and in his affections till the sun of grace and truth rises upon him. When, exactly, and just how, exactly, the sun of grace and truth rose upon our philosopher he does not tell us with any particularity. But what he does tell us most explicitly and most emphatically is this, as soon as that heavenly sun did arise upon him straightway all his original and inborn stupidity toward divine things began to melt away. Till as time went on, and as that all-enlightening sun rose higher and higher in his sky, he came more and more to see and to feel and to confess the presence of the most momentous of realities where before his conversion he had been quite content with so many ignorant and idle words. And till he makes this great confession in this autobiographical utterance of his: Verba in res—that is to say, with all his philosophical attainments, and with all his literary successes in some other departments of life and of thought, he had been all the time but a brutish man before God in the great things of God and in the great things of his own immortal soul. That philosopher's conversion manifested itself and proved itself true in more ways than one. But the one thing on which he here dwells is the fact that his hitherto idle words became, henceforth, the greatest of all realities to him.

Well, then, in proof and in illustration of our philosopher's great change, let us take the greatest of all words and the greatest of all realities first, and that is, GOD, ALMIGHTY GOD HIMSELF. At one time and for a long time this was the way in which this unconverted philosopher spoke and wrote concerning his Maker, Almighty God. These were some of his philosophical and literary names for Almighty God. God, to him, was the Great First Cause; He was the Ens entium. He was the Anima mundi; He was the Supreme Being; He was the Power behind phenomena; He was the Power, not ourselves, that makes for righteousness, and so on. But as God would have it, our philosopher came to see that all these names were so many idle words in his mind and in his heart and in his life. And till, after his conversion, he came to speak and to write on this greatest of all subjects in this truly noble and truly philosophical way. I speak now, he would say, of the God of the true theist. And I believe and I say that He is the God of truth, and of wisdom, and of love, and of righteousness, and of holiness. Moreover, He is omnipresent, omnipotent, invisible, incomprehensible. These are some of the distinctive prerogatives that I now ascribe, unconditionally and unreservedly, to the Great Being whom I call God. But as time still went on with our now theistic philosopher he came to see that while all these names and descriptions of God were not unscriptural, nor idle, nor invalid for his and other men's philosophical and apologetical and polemical purposes, yet for his own soul's salvation he was compelled to fall back, like the most unlearned and unphilosophical of believers, on that great Name of God which God Himself proclaimed to Moses, and the proclamation of which name made Moses make haste to fall down and pray. This Name: the LORD, the LORD God, merciful, and gracious, and long-suffering, and abundant in goodness, and in truth, forgiving iniquity, transgression, and sin. And, till our philosopher would say a hundred times every day—They who know this Name of Thine, they will put their trust in Thee.

Take the angel's injunction to Joseph as a second

result of our philosopher's conversion. "Thou shalt call His Name JESUS: for He shall save His people from their sins." Luther is always denouncing the "rotten pulpiteers" of his day who preached to their people an historical Gospel only. Now our philosopher, to begin with, knew the historical Jesus only, as he called Him; and from that historical name he preached, like Luther's rotten pulpiteers, an historical Gospel only. For many years he treated that great name JESUS very much as he treated that not small name Socrates. Now and then he would break out and would expatiate on the Socratic method of Jesus, as he called it. And from that he would with great eloquence extol the more-than-Socratic morality of Jesus, and would urge all men, and all young men especially, to imitate the walk and the conversation of Jesus. Only all the time in a historical, philosophical, and ethical way. But after his conversion all that critical and literary appreciation of Jesus, and all that philosophical patronage of his Divine Redeemer, came to an end. He no longer talked of his Divine Redeemer as the Founder of the Christian religion. Instead of that he soon had the angel's message to Joseph engraved verbatim on his watch-seal, and inscribed in gold letters upon all his writing-paper. Like John Bunyan at one time, our philosopher could not away with Paul; but after his great change came to him he could not put up with any of the apostles but Paul. And till, like Paul and Luther and Bunyan, our transformed philosopher would know nothing, neither in his philosophy nor in his theology nor in his ethic, but Jesus Christ, and Him crucified.

And there was this great change also. No one word in all his philosophical and ethical vocabulary took on such depth, and such inwardness, and such spirituality as did that formerly so idle word, sin. To him the sinfulness of sin, the unspeakable abominableness and horribleness of sin, ever after his full conversion, completely drank up all his former philosophy and morality. He seemed now to have no time left and no taste and no talent and no intellectual capacity of any kind for any study but his sleepless study of his own sin, and, over against his own sin, God's salvation. But then this utter abandonment and this complete absorption amply repaid him even intellectually and philosophically. For it supplied him with the true and the only key to all the deepest mysteries of God and man; and especially to all the deepest mysteries of good and evil in the mind of man, and in the heart of man, and in the personal and corporate life of all mankind. And, ever more and more, he had the sure verification of all that in his own mind, and in his own heart, every day. I am privileged to be able to give you a passage of his that he wrote on this all-commanding subject of his some time after his complete conversion. That so characteristic passage runs somewhat thus : " Unless we have some true and just idea of the state of our own hearts, we can have no true and just idea of a Saviour and a Sanctifier. Unless we know ourselves just as we are, a Saviour and a Sanctifier are both but idle words to us. It is exactly in proportion as we watch ourselves and search our own hearts, and there see something of the awful infection and deadly malady of our innermost nature; it is only so that we shall ever understand one single syllable of the Gospel. To startle men and to put them upon the true knowledge of themselves, that is the first function of the Christian pulpit as the Holy Ghost has set up the Christian pulpit among mankind. The doctrines of grace," he concludes, " are so many idle words to a man till he has seen and accepted himself as a lost and hopeless sinner." What a change, you will say, his conversion has produced upon that at one time so shallow-souled and so superficial philosopher!

Yes, indeed; but it is high time to come home to ourselves. And in coming home to ourselves let us follow in that philosopher's footsteps in order to see if we can keep step with him in and after his conversion. And first, take his experience in connection with that greatest of all names—the Name of GOD. Now what is your own experience in connection with that greatest of all Names? Our philosopher was not wholly wrong when he said that to him God was the Great First Cause; the Ens entium; the Anima mundi; the Supreme Being. And much more was he right when he came to see and to say that God is Truth Itself, Wisdom Itself, Love Itself, Righteousness Itself, Holiness Itself. But he was still more right and still more wise and still more reverent when he held his peace altogether and let God speak for Himself. And when, like Moses on the Mount, he made haste to his knees as soon as these divine words fell on his ears from God's own mouth: these divine words: Merciful, and gracious, and long-suffering, and abundant in goodness and in truth, forgiving iniquity, transgression, and sin. Now is all that the Name of God to you? Does your religious experience answer to God's own description of Himself? Speaking philosophically, has God's Covenant Name verified Itself, and demonstrated Itself, and vindicated Itself in you? What was at one time the idlest of words and the emptiest of names to you: is that Name now your first name every new morning, and your last name every returning night? Is that Name now your daily meat and your daily drink? Is that Name now your one song in the house of your pilgrimage? What is His Name and what is His Son's Name in your present experience, and in your converted philosophy?

And, then, as regards sin and especially as regards your own sinfulness. Have you ever had any experience like that of our great English philosopher, Samuel Taylor Coleridge? On the margin of a copy of Thomas Adams' "Private Thoughts," now preserved among the treasures of the British Museum, Coleridge has written these pencilled lines: "For a great part of my life I did not know that I was like Laodicea: wretched, and miserable, and poor, and blind, and naked. And even after I did discover that, I did not feel it aright. But I thank God that I feel all that, somewhat, now. I was deceived about my true self for a large part of my life by the sayings of some so-called philosophers, and by some scraps of poor poetry, but most of all by the pride of my own heart. The whole design of the Gospel of Jesus Christ is to discover men's hearts, and to change their views, and to change their tempers, and to change their whole lives. Yes! but how? By the superior excellence of its precepts? By the weight of its exhortations? By its promises, or by its rewards? No! No! But by convincing men of their utter wretchedness, their terrible guilt, and their absolute blindness to their sinful condition. And then by promising to the penitent sinner, and by actually conveying to him, all the blessings of the evangelical covenant." Well might Charles Lamb exclaim, "Reader! lend all thy books to S. T. C. For he will return them to thee with ample usury on the margin. I have had experience of him; and I counsel thee, shut not the door of thy heart, nor the door of thy library, against S. T. C."

Speaking of Coleridge, that great philosophical magician of words and names, recalls to my mind a story that John Newton tells to Thomas Scott in the Cardiphonia correspondence. A clerical friend of Newton's had for many years given but a cold superficial consent to the things of the Gospel. But as God would have it, Newton's friend was reading one day in the third chapter of Paul's Epistle to the Ephesians when his reading was arrested by that word $\dot{a}\nu\epsilon\xi\iota\chi\nu\iota\alpha\sigma\tau o\nu$—the unsearchable riches in the eighth verse. The Apostle, he said to himself, sometimes employs most remarkable words, as here, when he writes of the riches that are laid up in Christ. He speaks of heights, and of depths, and of lengths, and of breadths, and of things that are unsearchable. Now, I have found nothing in Christ that is not quite plain to me, and wholly natural, and and wholly rational. Surely Paul's experience of Christ and of Christ's riches must have been very different from my experience! And that one word in the third of the Ephesians was the beginning of a study of Paul that ended in that preacher's complete conversion. And till both he and Thomas Scott became two of the most illustrious examples of this great evangelical law—Verba in res—great words changed into great realities.

Now during this whole discussion this arresting question may well have arisen in some men's hearts, Are they converted themselves? Philosopher or no, wise man or foolish, learned man or ignorant, am I a converted man or am I not? Has that great change, up to this day, taken place in me? some humble-minded man may be asking himself at this moment. Well, sir, these are some of the infallible marks of a truly converted man—these: Have you ever, definitely and abidingly, accepted the Son of God as your Saviour from sin and death and hell? And especially from sin? Have you ever consciously and deliberately submitted yourself to be justified by God and before God by the suretyship and imputed righteousness of Jesus Christ? Or, again, have you this apostolic proof that you have passed from death to life, that you love the brethen? Or, again, is your treasure now at last laid up in heaven? Or, once again, do you ever, for Christ's sake, visit the fatherless and widows in their affliction? And, if you still suspect yourself, and wish to make yourself doubly sure where you have so much at stake, then add on to all these scriptural marks of a true conversion this experimental mark of this converted philosopher. Recall and keep in memory all you have been told about him this morning: about his change of mind concerning the Name of God, and concerning Jesus Christ, and concerning himself, and concerning his own sinfulness. Start a conversation at table to-day about Coleridge and Charles Lamb, and who can tell but that conversation may help forward some domestic conversion, say of your University son, that is more on your mind than even your own. Recall also the Cardiphonia anecdote; and you might purchase a copy of that classic and make a present of it to some young minister. And almost more than all that, keep your eye on yourself when you are invited to sing or to hear sung such converted songs as these. When "Just as I am" is sung, examine yourself and see if you instinctively and immediately gather up all your present life, just as you are, and put it all, on the spot, into that great song of faith and prayer to the Lamb of God. Again, when you sing "There is a Fountain," do you all the time plunge yourself and out of sight under the stream of blood and water that flows over you from Immanuel's veins? And again, when John Newton leads you in this:—

> Jesus ! my Shepherd, Husband, Friend,
> My Prophet, Priest, and King,
> My Lord, my Life, my Way, my End,
> Accept the praise I bring.

Watch yourself whether or no you bring any praise to Him that He will accept. Ask yourself if there is any reality now in your once idle words about His being your Shepherd, and your Husband, and your Friend, and your Lord, and your Life, and your Way, and your End. And if you can intelligently and honestly and experimentally say that these are no longer idle words with you, then, if you follow on in that way, there can be no shadow of doubt that your conversion will be held to be valid on that Day : on that Day, when, as Newman had it put on his epitaph, " Ex umbris et imaginibus in veritatem." That is to say, when you like him shall have escaped from this world of idle words and the shadows of things, and shall have risen away up into that great world where all truth and all reality and all righteousness and all love shall for ever dwell.

XIII

SO THEN

TO begin with,—what exactly does this little word " so " mean in the text? This little word " so " as it comes to us from Paul's pen at the close of the most experimental and the most pungent passage the Apostle ever wrote—what does it really mean? Let us ask that question at the previous context, and at our own hearts, till we get a satisfactory answer to it. For this so innocent-looking little word will be sure to elude us and deceive us unless we arrest it and put it under pressure so as to compel it to yield up to us the whole of Paul's mind in penning it. But when we do put this so elusive little word under sufficient pressure, and when we bestow sufficient scrutiny upon it, we come to see that, small as it is, this little word sums up into itself the deepest experiences of the deepest-souled man, the most spiritually-minded man, and the most heavenly-minded man that ever lived. Yes; this one little word " so " here sums up, and puts into the smallest of syllables, the whole of the foregoing chapter, which is the deepest the most heart-searching and the most heartbroken chapter that ever was written since writing was.

For one thing, this little word "so" contains within itself all this. Putting his whole life before his conversion into his own so vivid and so powerful words, Paul tells us that he was at one time "alive without the law." He was what he calls alive as long as the holy law of God remained wholly outside of his inward life. But when the law of God, in all its intense spirituality, really penetrated into Paul's mind, and heart, and conscience, and imagination, then he died—died, he means, to all his previous self-righteousness, self-satisfaction, self-complacency, self-importance, and to all peace with God and with himself. To all that Paul was henceforth as good as a dead man. When the holy law of God really entered Paul's conscience and demanded of him that on pain of death and hell he must not covet what any other man possesses, nor envy any other man, nor hate any other man, nor have any ill-will at any other man, nor think, nor speak, nor do against any other man what he would not like to have thought or spoken or done against himself—that so holy, so spiritual, and so heart-searching law of God he found to be absolutely death and hell to him. You all understand that, I am sure. At any rate, as many of you as have come through that same heart-searching and heart-breaking experience; and especially as many of you as are passing more and more through that same heart-searching and heart-breaking experience every day you live.

Then, again, "sold under sin,"—that is another terrible experience and terrible expression of the

Apostle. Sold under that cruellest and hatefullest of all slave-driving masters. And then this wonderful saint and wonderful writer proceeds to open up to all his like-minded readers his own innermost experience as a slave sold under sin. Like a sold slave Paul pants to be free. But he soon finds that perfect freedom from the tyranny of his indwelling sin is absolutely impossible to him. A slave's will is free. No master, the most tyrannical, can chain up a slave's will; while all the time his hands and his feet are bound fast in fetters of iron. But no fetters were ever rivetted on any slave's hands and feet that he so hated, and so cursed, and so kicked against as Paul hated, and cursed, and kicked against those fetters of indwelling sin under the cruel dominion of which he so continually agonized. Yes, great thanks be to God, Paul's will is free. As our Pauline Catechism—the most Pauline of all the catechisms—has it, in our effectual calling our minds are savingly enlightened, and our wills are savingly renewed. Now, Paul's will was savingly renewed in his effectual calling—savingly renewed as, I suppose, no other man's mind and will have ever been so savingly renewed. But not yet his heart; not yet his whole heart; not yet his whole spirit and disposition and inclination and affection. Paul's whole will was now wholly set upon always thinking and feeling and wishing what was good, both toward God and toward all men. But with all that there were still the remains of his original sin lurking deep down in his imperfectly sanctified heart. And thus it was that his better mind and better will were so often forerun and forestalled; overrun and overborne by the uprush of the inward sinfulness that still dwelt deep down within him. In the most heart-breaking chapter that ever was written in this world the greatest writer in this world displays to us the supreme tragedy of this world—that is to say, his sanctified mind and will everlastingly warring within him against his still unrenewed heart—everlastingly warring within him till he is the wretchedest man on the face of the earth; just because in his mind and in his will he is the holiest of men.

And again, mark this, and mark all that follows from this: Again and again and again Paul tells us that he "finds" all that to be the constant case within himself. Paul's indwelling sin and its accursed slavery was not a doctrine that he had been taught in any school, Jewish or Christian. For lessons in the doctrine of original and indwelling sin Paul had not sat at any man's feet: prophet, nor psalmist, nor apostle. Whether they all taught that doctrine or not he does not stop to say. But what he does say, and with all his might, is this: that indwelling sin is not a doctrine at all to him. No; to him it is a sure experience. It is not even a divine doctrine to him, so much as a spiritual and a personal experience: a daily, a bitter, a hateful, a loathsome, a cruel, and a lifelong spiritual experience. "And then, among other things," says John Owen, that most Pauline of men, "this inward experience of Paul is the great guarantee and the sure preservative of evangelical truth in Paul's mind, and heart, and doctrine; just as it is in every man's mind, and heart, and doctrine who has Paul's spiritual experience." No man need attempt to argue Paul—no, nor any of Paul's successors—out of this so experimental and so personal truth, because they all "find" it in themselves. Incontestably so, according to the depth and the sincerity and the spirituality of their minds and their hearts. 'I know it,' says the Apostle. 'I know it, beyond all possible dispute or shadow of doubt. For I find it within my own soul, continually and incessantly, and that to my cost, to my shame, and to my deepest pain; to a shame and to a pain that are simply indescribable and inconsolable.' "Some," says John Owen, summing up his great masterpiece on this deep matter—"some pretend to great natural virtue, and some to great gospel perfection, but I am resolved to believe the Apostle and my own experience." And so am I.

"So, then, with the mind I myself serve the law of God, but with the flesh the law of sin." That is to say, since all that is "so" with me, Paul, and since all that has been so with me ever since my conversion—and is not less so, but is every new day more so—"then" let me penitently and contritely, and humbly, and resignedly make up my mind and lay my account with all my divinely ordained condition in this life. Let me take up this awful inward cross of mine; let me endure to the end this cruellest of all thorns of mine, and follow after the holy law of God, if with ever-bleeding feet, till the end comes. And let me believe and be

H

sure that His grace is sufficient for me, and that His strength will be made perfect in all my weakness. Let me live ever near the fountain opened for such awful uncleanness as mine, and keep my heart ever open to His holy and indwelling Spirit till the day dawns when He shall unloose all my remaining bonds, and give me my full and everlasting discharge from this terrible battle. All that, and much more than all that, is summed up in these two all-containing words of Paul: "So, then." "So, then, with the mind, I myself serve the law of God, but with the remainders of the flesh the law of sin."

Now, my brethren, my Pauline-minded brethren, be you few or many this morning, carrying all that with us, let us come home to ourselves. And as Paul has here written his most inward, most secret, and most spiritual experience for our learning—for our best learning—let us honestly and courageously imitate him and read out our own spiritual experience to ourselves and to one another. And, accordingly, if you will accompany me, I will now read out to you some of your own most inward and most painful, but at the same time, most spiritual and most soul-sanctifying experiences—yours and mine. And, since Paul is so nobly plain-spoken about himself, let me err on the same side, with you and with myself.

Well, then, there are certain men planted by God's special appointment all around you and me. Paul does not name his God-planted and God-appointed men and neither will I name yours nor mine. But they are there. And I am sure that we often name them to ourselves and to God, as Paul often did. Men whom we do not love and who do not love us; men whom we have hurt and who have hurt us; men who stand in our way and oppose and hinder and obstruct us; men who possess name and fame and place and honour and reward that we would fain possess, and so on and so on, in this whole world of such unceasing trial and temptation. And as often as we read or hear the names of those men, as often as we pass their doors and windows, as often as we meet them, or any of theirs on the street, like Paul's evil heart, our evil heart rises up in enmity and in malice against them. But the next moment our will, our renewed and sanctified will, denounces our evil heart and refuses to join with our evil heart in its evil ways. Now, at that enslaved moment ours is a case of what the old experimental divines were wont to call *motus primi non cadunt sub libertatem*. That is to say, the first motions of sin in our evil heart do not come under the jurisdiction of our will. But to make up for that, as far as may be, our renewed will rises up immediately and repudiates our evil heart, and immediately proceeds against it, and in this way. The very next moment after that sudden uprush of indwelling sin from our heart our better will turns to God on the spot—on the very street sometimes—and cries to Him for instantaneous pardon and for a clean heart. Aye, and more than all that, far more than all that, and far more well-pleasing to God than all that—we protest to Him as He is our Witness and our Judge that, if

He will only put it in our power to do that enemy of ours a service—him, or any of his—we swear to God that we will immediately and rejoicingly do it. Now, that was Paul's case exactly at the moment when he was penning his seventh chapter to the Romans. And so much is our case the same as his was, that if he had omitted to pen that chapter to the saints at Rome, by the same Spirit and out of the same experience we would have penned it for ourselves. For we know, quite as well as Paul knew, that the law is spiritual, but that we, in many things, are still inwardly sinful, and are as much sold under sin as ever he was.

I have kept you too long already, I fear, on this not very easy and not very pleasant and not very acceptable argument. But if you will bear with me I have still a few words I would like to say. For one thing, you will be glad to be told that this deep spiritual experience of the Apostle is not confined to Calvinists and Puritans such as I have named. Take our old Bible-class friend, Santa Teresa, for one. I open her classical autobiography and I read this: " God leads His people in the way He chooses out as the best for them and for His special purposes with them individually. Whom the Lord specially loveth He layeth on them His special cross. And the heaviest of all His special crosses is a life of sanctification and service without sensible consolation. It is indeed a very great misery to live on in this evil world where our deadly enemies are ever at our door, and where we can neither eat nor sleep nor work nor rest in peace, but are compelled to have our armour on night and day. There is no rest nor happiness here, nor will be till we are home with the everlastingly Blessed. As I write," she says, "I am seized with terror lest I should never escape this sinful life. I know one who often wishes for death in order that she may be freed from the torment of her sinful heart. Her fear is not so much of hell as that she should so grieve God's Holy Spirit that He will be wearied out with her and so forsake her and leave her in her sins." The Catholic saint does not in so many words mention the seventh of the Romans, but I can see that every verse of it is deep down in her mind and in her heart, as it was in the mind and heart of an old Puritan saint lately gone to his rest, whose extended pilgrimage was over ninety years, and who often said that he must have been often swallowed up of despair had it not been for the seventh chapter of Paul's Epistle to the Romans.

Now, my more thoughtful brethren, arising out of all that, it has been a great problem with all the greatest saints and with all the deepest divines in all ages—this great problem : Why is it that the Holy Spirit so leaves the seventh of the Romans, more or less, in the souls of all the truly regenerate ? Why is it that He takes them all through this terrible experience, more or less ? Now, what would you say toward the solution of that great problem ? For you must be studying that great problem, many of you, more than any other problem on the face of the earth. Well, what do you say to it ? Are you getting any light upon God's mind and will with you in this so mysterious matter? Can you at all justify and vindicate Him when He is judged and blamed in this so perplexing and so painful matter? Are you learning anything about the deepest of all God's ways with His saints as these years of such spiritual suffering go on with you? There is an old proverb to this effect, that experience teaches, even fools. Well, is your experience teaching you anything worth calling teaching? There is more than a proverb in this of Paul in his eighth chapter that all things work together for good. And the Apostle does not exclude from that law even your indwelling sin. Well, look down into your own sinful heart and see. And I will say this concerning some of you, with some personal experience of what I say: Is not your indwelling sin teaching you lessons about itself, lessons that you could never have learned but from itself? Is not your indwelling, tyrannizing, enslaving sin teaching you lessons concerning its power and its persistence and its depth and its malignity and its absolutely unspeakable wickedness—lessons and experiences that break your heart every day you live? And anything and everything that breaks your heart every day is good—indeed, is your best good—in this present life. And that because the sacrifices of God, the every morning and the every night sacrifices of God, are a broken heart. And, then, is not this so also—that with your daily broken hearts you are putting on every day a new humility and a new patience with God and with all men and with yourselves? As, also, an ever new prayerful-ness, and an ever new faith in Christ and an ever new love for the word of God and for spiritual reading and spiritual preaching? And, above all, far, far above all—Jesus Christ Himself is beginning to get His right place with you and within you. A place He would never have got but for your indwelling sin.

This is Goodwin's winding up :—

"When the Apostle, long after his first conversion, was in the midst of that great and famous battle chronicled in the seventh of Romans, presently upon that woeful outcry, O wretched man that I am! he falls admiring the grace of justification through Christ. Now, he says, there is no condemnation to them that are in Christ. Mark that word *now*: that now, after such bloody wounds and gashes, there should be no condemnation, this exceedingly exalts the grace of justification. For if ever, thought he, I was in danger of condemnation it was upon the rising and the rebelling of those my corruptions. But I find, says he, that God still pardons me, and accepts me as much as ever upon my returning to Him. Now this is a Gospel indeed."

And this is the winding up of Walter Marshall, Goodwin's greatest disciple: "Let us observe and consider diligently in our whole conversation that though we are partakers of a holy state by faith in Christ, yet our natural state doth remain, in a measure, with all its corrupt principles and properties. Therefore, we must be content to leave the natural man in us vile and wicked, as we found it, until it is utterly abolished by death. . . . And all this serveth to work self-loathing, and self-abasement, and to make us look upon nature as desperately wicked, and not to be reformed but by putting on Christ. It remains wicked, and only wicked, even after we have put on Christ, though we must not allow its wickedness, but rather groan to be delivered from the body of this death, thanking God that there is a deliverance through Jesus Christ our Lord."

XIV

MOTUS PRIMI NON CADUNT SUB LIBERTATEM

THE seventh of the Romans was not written for babes at the breast. Paul wrote this terrible chapter for the use and for the comfort of all those men to the end of time and to the end of sin who should come, like himself, to know something of the plague of their own hearts. Everyone that useth milk is unskilful in the word of righteousness, for he is a babe. But strong meat belongeth to them that are of full age; even to those who, by reason of use, have their senses exercised to discern both good and evil. In the seventh of the Romans we read of an agony of soul the like of which is nowhere to be read again in all human history, sacred or profane. This is the tragedy of all tragedies. All the other tragedies that we anywhere read of are but so much child's play compared with this tragedy. The very greatest of them all compared with Paul's tragedy are but so much sound and fury, signifying nothing.

Motus primi non cadunt sub libertatem. Now that is just so much old evangelical Latin for the seventh of the Romans. And the graphic old Latin will greatly help us to enter into those spiritual experiences that Paul has recorded for us in this the experimentally profoundest of all his Epistles. *Motus primi*—that is to say, the first motions of sin in the soul, *non cadunt sub libertatem*—do not come under the jurisdiction, no, nor always under the cognisance of the regenerate will. That exactly describes the Apostle's deepest experience every day of his regenerate and spiritual life, and he was led of the Holy Spirit to put his experience into that terrible chapter for the instruction and for the consolation of all truly spiritually-minded and all truly sin-exercised men to the end of time.

As Paul's wonderful life went on; as God more and more revealed His Son in Paul; and as the Apostle grew more and more in personal holiness and in true spirituality of mind, he came to look at himself more and more in this way, and in this light. He came to see that the original stuff, so to call it; the original substance, etymologically speaking, out of which his whole inner man was made,—by some awful aboriginal catastrophe, that substance had all been poisoned with sin, somehow, from the first moment of its existence. The very protoplasm, so to call it, out of which Paul's whole inward man had been made, was already tainted and vitiated in every original atom of it. And that before his soul had been drawn out and developed into his mind and will and conscience and affections and emotions. And thus it was that all those faculties and powers and operations of Paul's soul were all already corrupted and poisoned at their root and source and spring long before they had come into his keeping. To his unspeakable horror Paul discovered all that within himself as soon as the scales really fell off his eyes; and he discovered all that, more and more, as his eyes were more and more opened to the awful sinfulness that dwelt, unceasingly and inexpugnably, deep down in the depths of his soul. And thus it was that long after his new birth from above,—aye, long after he was the holiest man on earth,—his old and aboriginal sinfulness continued to taint, and to infect, and to corrupt, and to pollute all he thought and said and did, let him do his very best, and his very utmost, to be delivered from it. To take the Latin rendering of the text, long after Paul's will had been renewed, long after all his powers of voluntary choice had been rectified and strengthened by the Spirit of God; even so, the first motions of sin in his soul continued to be so deep, so secret, so sudden, and so strong, that every day he was ensnared and enslaved to sin, long before he was able to repudiate its evil motions, or to remonstrate against them, or to repress them, or to cast them out. And hence arose that awful captivity to sin under the agony of which he breaks out continually into these awful heart-breaks to God: O wretched man that I am! For, what I hate like hell I am every day swept away into doing, so sold am I, and so enslaved am I, to the sin that still dwelleth in me. O the wretchedest of all men that I am! Who shall deliver me from the body of this death?

Now, as regards the total inability even of the regenerate will to rule and to restrain the first sinful motions of the soul we have a great cloud of spiritually-minded witnesses from Paul's day down to our own day. A great cloud of witnesses composed of all men of real depth of mind and of real spiritual experience and spiritual insight. Dante, for instance, has this on the powerlessness of the will to command and to rule the emotions :—

> The Mantuan, when he heard him, turned to me,
> And, holding silence, by his countenance
> Enjoined me silence ; but the power that wills
> Bears not supreme control: laughter and tears
> Follow so closely on the passion prompts them,
> They wait not for the motions of the will
> In natures most sincere.

And Luther, the most Paul-like man in all our modern world, is far better and far deeper on this spiritual subject than even Dante himself. " Concerning inward sinfulness," says Luther, " there is no mortal man in whom it does not dwell. Paul, that most holy Apostle, bitterly confessed it. He longed to be free from the secret motions of sin in his soul ; but he never was free from those motions as long as he lived in the flesh. I myself," says the great Reformer, " labour and pray to be freed from my indwelling sin ; but I can never attain to that freedom for which I fight. Old Adam still dwells in me, and will dwell in me, till I rise in the resurrection, and leave him for ever behind me in my grave. He is a true Christian who feels bitterly that he is a great sinner, and who hates himself on that account; and who strives against his sinfulness with all his mind and will, all his might and main. And he is no true Christian who thinks that he has no secret sinfulness. You will know all true Christians," says Luther, " by their continual shriek, Who shall deliver me from the body of this death ? " And John Owen, in his masterly treatise on this same subject, has this: " Often, before a man is aware, and that without any outward temptation, his indwelling sin will rise up secretly in his heart and will set all his inward world on fire. Often, when a man is engaged upon quite another design, sin suddenly starts up in his heart, and carries his whole soul into a guilty and miserable state. And," this great Puritan sums up, " I know no greater burden in the life of a believer than just these involuntary surprisals of his soul; involuntary as to the actual consent of his will." And John Bunyan has put all that in his own inimitable and never-to-be-be-forgotten way : " One thing I would not let slip. I took notice that now poor Christian was so confounded that he did not know his own voice, and thus I perceived it. Just when he was come over against the mouth of the burning pit, one of the wicked ones got behind him, and stepped up softly to him, and, whisperingly, suggested many grievous blasphemies to him which he verily thought had proceeded from his own mind. This put Christian more to it than anything he had met with before, even to think that he should now blaspheme Him that he loved so much before. Yet if he could have helped he would not have done it; but he had not the discretion to shut his ears, nor to know from whence those blasphemies came."

Now, my brethren, that is not the sad estate of Paul and Luther and John Owen and John Bunyan only. All that is in us all, whether we have made that sad discovery in ourselves or no; deep down in your soul and in my soul all that sad state of things is going on within us every day. Aye, and is going on in the very best of us, before we are aware that there is anything wrong with us. "Original sin," as Augustine first named it: that supreme mystery of iniquity, is to be found working out its woefulness in every one of us every hour of every day. Hundreds of times every day there are deep and deadly motions of sin in all our souls, whether we recognise them and resist them or no. Secret entrails of original sin are seething and festering in the depths of our souls, such as anger, and envy, and jealousy, and hatred, and malice, and ill-will, and desire for revenge; and, again, a sleepless self-seeking and self-pleasing, and self-exalting, and all manner of self-will. An ever-craving lust for praise, and for honour, and for promotion; secret stirrings of envy and jealousy at our best friends who are prospering better than we are; or, even, that they should prosper at all; a deep-down anger at some offence we have taken; at some bitterly resented correction or contradiction we have received; or at some slight or some disparagement we have suffered at someone's hands; or, again, involuntary and unaccountable uprushes of gloom and sullenness and sourness of soul; of pride, and scorn, and contempt, and resentment. A certain man, whose name we could give you, once injured us, or we think he did. He spoke against us, or he wrote against us, or he voted against us; he crossed our wishes; he thwarted our plans; he shipwrecked our hopes. That was a week ago; it was a month ago; it was ten years ago; it was twenty years ago; but at the bottom of our hearts we have never forgiven him nor any of his. We never read or hear his name; we never meet him or any of his on the street; no, nor even at the church door, that our old hatred at him does not surge up in our hearts. And that, though we have repeatedly done him good and spoken him good during all those years, and have never once done or spoken him evil, or without repenting of it. But, all the time, it is the seventh of the Romans over again in ourselves. We may never have learned Latin but all the same this is that Latin proverb fufilled in us: *Motus primi non cadunt sub libertatem*. It was this same discovery of himself that made David sob out to all time that he had been conceived in sin and had been shapen in iniquity. And Isaiah, that his whole head was sick and his whole heart faint and that he was undone. And Jeremiah, that his heart was deceitful above all things, and desperately wicked. And Daniel, that all his comeliness was turned within him into corruption. And Paul to pen the seventh of the Romans. And a multitude that no man can number to confess all these things concerning themselves down to this day; aye, down to this morning hour in this house.

But someone—with some real anxiety, and, perhaps, with some real anger—will demand of me, are there then no good motions at all in our human hearts? O yes, sir! O yes! Thank God there often are! There are often such secret and deep-down motions in our hearts as these. There are often original motions of love, and joy, and peace, and long-suffering, and gentleness, and goodness, and faith, and meekness, and temperance, and many such-like stirrings of the life of God in the depth of our souls. Yes, often, thank God. And when these good motions come up out of the depths of our souls and find a renewed will waiting to receive and assist them in the upper regions of our souls, then these good motions become far more than mere motions. For they immediately fill our whole soul with sweet and holy and heavenly affections toward God and man. And with the assistance of our renewed wills they soon cover our whole life with works of righteousness and true holiness. Only, you must understand that the seventh of the Romans and its Latin parallel are taken up with a class of cases, the sad opposite of such happy cases as these.

A whole crowd of lessons and counsels here press hard upon me to utter them. But I am compelled confine myself to two or three at the most.

Well, take this for one lesson.

Paul himself was a proud-hearted, hard-hearted, cruel-hearted Pharisee, till the scales fell off his eyes. But as soon as the scales fell off his eyes he became the chief of sinners, and the most broken-hearted believer in the whole Church of Christ. Downcast soul! be thankful for this at any rate, that the scales have fallen off your eyes. The rest of Paul's experience will more and more follow to you. And Luther, our modern Paul, was wont to say in his reformation, and evangelical, sermons that to see sin in a man's own soul is to see very hell itself. And that the only hell that gave him any concern was the hell he carried about with him in the bottomless pit of his own evil heart. And John Owen, the great English Calvinist, was wont to say that the heaviest cross a Christian man has to carry in this world is a heart full of involuntary sin. Be of good cheer, O broken-hearted believers. Paul, and Luther, and Owen are all now with Christ, and are, for ever, like Him in their deepest hearts. And you will be with them before very long; you will soon be with them and will be for ever like them. Be of good cheer.

And, meantime, steep your mind and your memory; nay, saturate your whole soul continually in every part of it with Holy Scripture. Pour down every day into the depths of your evil heart Gospel doctrines and Gospel promises, with a constant stream of psalms, and hymns, and spiritual songs, till the first motions of your deepest heart shall be motions no longer of the poison of sin, but, instead of that, the motions of prayer, and praise, and faith, and hope, and love, and holiness. Let your every day and every hour prayer to God be Thomas Ken's every day and every hour prayer: Say and sing with Ken continually:—

> Guard my first springs of thought and will,
> And with Thyself my spirit fill.

And if you have passed for ever out of your intellectual and spiritual childhood, be thankful, then, with all far-advanced saints; be very thankful for the seventh of the Romans. As already reported, "it was the saying of an eminent man of God, lately gone to his rest, whose extended pilgrimage was over ninety-three years, that he would often have been swallowed up of despair, had it not been for the seventh chapter of Paul's Epistle to the Romans."

And all you who are so covered with the shame and pain of your inward sinfulness that you can look neither God nor man nor yourself in the face, I have a parting word from evangelical Isaiah for you. "For all your shame, and for all your pain, you shall yet have double. And for your confusion you shall yet rejoice in your portion. Therefore, in your land you shall possess the double; and everlasting joy shall be upon your head." The consul Agrippa was shut up in a cruel and loathsome prison for Gaius's sake. But no sooner did Gaius ascend the throne than he had his friend instantly released and conferred upon him an office both of great riches and of great renown. Moreover, Gaius presented Agrippa with a chain of gold double the weight of the chain of iron that he had worn in the prison for Gaius's sake. And so has Paul's ascended and enthroned Lord done long ago for His holy Apostle. And so will He do before very long for you also. For you, that is, who are sold under sin for His Name's sake, and for your own sanctification's sake. For all your shame, and for all your pain, and for all your self-loathing, you shall then possess far more than the double. For, with His own hand Christ will hang a chain of everlasting salvation around your neck; a chain of everlasting salvation that will make you to forget for ever all the unspeakably sad years of your Paul-like captivity to your indwelling sin.

> He comes! the pris'ners to relieve,
> In Satan's bondage held;
> The gates of brass before him burst,
> The iron fetters yield.
>
> He comes! the broken hearts to bind,
> The bleeding souls to cure;
> And with the treasures of His grace
> T' enrich the humble poor.

Even so: come quickly, Lord Jesus.

No, indeed! Paul did not write the seventh of the Romans for babes at the breast.

Writes John Newton in a letter to Thomas Scott before Scott's eyes were opened: "Your comment on the seventh of the Romans contradicts my feelings. You are either of a different make and nature from me, or else you are not yet rightly apprised of your own state, if you do not find the Apostle's complaints to be very suitable to yourself. I believe that chapter to be applicable to the most holy Christian upon earth." And I will add, to no other.

XV

A SQUEEZE OF THE FORBIDDEN FRUIT

THE very first squeeze of the forbidden fruit produced shame and fear and cowardice and self-excusing in the Garden of Eden. Adam, where art thou? I heard Thy voice in the garden, and I was afraid, and I hid myself. Hast thou eaten of the tree whereof I commanded thee that thou shouldest not eat? And Adam said, The woman Thou gavest to be with me, she gave me of the tree, and I did eat. And the Lord God said to the woman, What is this that thou hast done? And the woman said, The serpent beguiled me, and I did eat. And thus it is that the first book of our Bible is called the Book of Genesis. The Genesis, that is, of man and of woman; of sin and its wages; and all already pointing on to the Book of the Generation of the Second Adam, who is both the Son of God and the seed of the woman, and whose name is Jesus Christ our Divine Redeemer.

Our best commentator on the Book of Genesis has this: " Now, in convincing a man of his fallen estate, I would not begin with the fall of Adam and Eve, I would begin with the man himself. With

A SQUEEZE OF THE FORBIDDEN FRUIT 133

the very man himself; as a poor, miserable, weak, vain, distressed, corrupt, selfish, self-tormenting creature. Let any man first enter into himself and read himself aright, and then he will read Moses and David and Christ and Paul with a true understanding, and with faith and comfort and hope." And, then, there is no real difference in this matter among all the generations of fallen men. God has seen good to make all mankind of one blood, and that one blood is the blood of Adam and Eve, with the original squeeze of their forbidden fruit inseparably mixed up with it. And that fountain-head taint of original sin has broken out in every new member of the human race in his own way. There is really no difference or only such differences as these: His special share in the original sin broke out in Cain in envy and murder; it broke out in Noah in intemperance; it broke out in Esau in religious indifference; it broke out in Jacob in avarice; it broke out in vanity and loquacity in Joseph; and it broke out in hatred and revenge in his brethren. And then, as David, of all Old Testament men, would seem to have known best the depth and the inveteracy of the corruption he had inherited; Behold, I was shapen in iniquity and in sin did my mother conceive me. He seems also to have known best in what his true remedy lay: Behold, thou desirest truth in my inward part, and in my hidden part thou shalt make me to know wisdom. The wisdom, that is, of knowing the inherited sinfulness of his own evil heart, and then the resulting wisdom of crying continually, Create in me a clean heart, O God, and renew a right spirit within me. Even so, my fallen brethren, your very best wisdom and mine will lie in our knowing just what exact deadly drop from the squeeze of the forbidden fruit has poisoned and corrupted our heart's blood. That will be our very best wisdom, because God desires and demands to see it in us. And because it always leads us on to Him who is the true Wisdom and the true Righteousness that God has provided for such fallen men as we are. Have we, then, because of some forbidden fruit of ours, any of that fear and shame that is recorded concerning our first parents? And, with that, have we any of that cowardice and self-excusing which they immediately exhibited? Again, have we any of Cain's evil heart in us? A heart that so envies and hates some brother of ours that we could take him out to the field and kill him? Or is our besetting sin that of Noah, or that of Esau, or that of Jacob, or that of Joseph, or that of his revengeful brethren? Or, alas! it may well be that *all* their several taints are in our own one blood, if not all their several trespasses in our own lives. Goodwin is always quoting the old Stoics—who taught their disciples that all the vices are within all men, though they have not yet all actually broken out in all men.

And then, out of a massive volume of some 500 pages on the squeezes of the forbidden fruit, Goodwin has a rich application of such lessons as these to his so highly privileged City Temple people,

1. And first, bending over his pulpit, with those soul-piercing eyes of his, the great preacher gave

A SQUEEZE OF THE FORBIDDEN FRUIT 135

his people this poignant lesson : " Single out," he said, " the grossest sin thou hast ever committed, the sin that brought thee lowest to thy knees, or that has cost thee a lifetime of a broken heart ; single out and compare that great sin with thy sinful heart, which was the cursed root out of which that cursed fruit grew. Take any poisonous root in thy garden, cut a piece out of it, and boil that piece in water, and you will find that there is far more essential poison in that root than there is in all the leaves and in all the fruits that have as yet sprung up out of that evil root." That lesson of Goodwin's always calls to my mind a similar lesson of Newman's :—

> Man lay a grovelling babe upon the ground,
>   Polluted in the blood of his first sire,
> With all his essence shattered and unsound,
>   And coiled around his heart a demon dire.
> O man, strange composite of heaven and earth :
>   Majesty dwarfed to baseness ! fragrant flower
> Running to poisonous seed ! and seeming worth
>   Clothing corruption, weakness mastering power !

Now, taking the great Puritan and the great Papist together, we get this lesson of thankfulness and of hope—this lesson : That if these two preachers, standing at the two poles of the Church of Christ, agree so scripturally and so experimentally in their foundation doctrines of the fall of man and of the fallen state of all mankind, may we not pray and hope that both their Churches will yet come to see eye to eye, and that not only on the first and Second Adam, but also on what our Catechism calls " the effectual application of the redemption purchased by Christ?" Let us pray for that promised time for modern Christendom and welcome every beginning of the answer to God's promise and to our prayer.

2. Another lesson that day was this: "As several men have their several employments, even so the God-Man hath His. And His own and special employment is to take the original squeeze of the forbidden fruit out of our blood, even as it was taken out of His own blood. And He is the one supreme specialist in this great operation. Therefore, if thou wouldest have thy heart's blood unpoisoned, purified, sweetened, and made blessed blood, you know to whom to apply. For that is His proper business. As if you would have some great work done, that never a man in all England could do it, you would send for a tradesman beyond sea: and so, when there was no one upon earth to do it, God sent to heaven for His Son to come down to do it."

3. And then, and so like himself, the great preacher does not let his people go home till he has impressed this Athanasian lesson upon them: "Though all the world complain not of the poison in its blood, yet do thou lay open thy bad heart before the throne of God every day, and do that as if no one else in all the world had such a bad heart as yours. Yes; daily and hourly. For, what is there that belongs to thee that hath anything unclean in it but you clean and cleanse daily and nightly and many times every day and night. Your hands and face; your clothes that do but hang

upon you; your house you live in you sweep and garnish daily; nay, your very streets that you walk in you cleanse weekly; and much more, surely, your own unclean and sin-festered heart, which will not let you breathe in purity and peace for a single hour." When Jacob Behmen's disciple asked him, " How shall I ever be able to keep my heart clean within me and my life without me ? " the Teutonic philosopher replied : " If thou dost once every hour throw thyself by faith beyond all creatures into the bottomless mercy of God, and into the sin-atoning sufferings of Christ, and into the fellowship of His intercession, thou shalt every hour receive power from above to rule over the world and death, and the devil and hell, and even over thy own heart itself. Aye, every half-hour," he added.

4. And then, from the daily experience he was himself having of the divine power and blessedness of the Puritan faith, Goodwin says : " My brethren, love and value your religion ! For, oh, how slightly, how slenderly, how leanly, and how dilutely do some so-called preachers speak of, and pass over, the greatest matters, and of the greatest concernment to mankind ! Let us take part rather with David and with Paul." And on the same day, and on the same subject, Thomas Halyburton was saying to his students at St Andrews : " Gentlemen, how I thank God that He ever made me a minister and a preacher of the Gospel as it is preached and received in Scotland ! " And I subscribe with all my heart to both Goodwin and Halyburton in this great matter.

And now the last lesson to any minister, and to any young minister especially who may have read these lines, is surely this: That Goodwin's tenth volume is the best book of true anthropology and true soteriology in all the world. Let them put aside all ephemeral and all impertinent books till they have mastered Goodwin, and see what their best people will say about their preaching. God bless you and them, is the prayer and benediction of a life-long student of Thomas Goodwin.

XVI

AN OUNCE OF THE GOLDEN CALF

IN his powerful treatise on Sin and its Punishment Thomas Goodwin tells us that to this day when any sore punishment falls upon a Jew, he always sees in it an ounce of the golden calf of his fathers. The origin of that ounce was this. Besides the jewels of gold and of silver that the children of Israel took out of Egypt they brought with them also no little of the licentious life and licentious practices of that corrupt land. As long as Moses stood at the head of the people their sensuality was restrained, but when their great leader left them to commune for a season with God on the mount, it broke out into a perfect saturnalia of open sin. And the calf of gold that Aaron, of all men, made wherewith to excite and, so to say, consecrate the licentiousness of the people,—on his return to the camp Moses in his hot anger took the filthy image and ground it to powder and strawed the powder upon the water, and made all the people to drink of it. As he said in his great sermon, " I took your sin, even the calf which ye had made, and I burnt it with fire, and stamped it, and ground it very small, even till it was as small as dust, and I cast the dust thereof into the brook that descended out of the mount." And hence that bitter proverb in the house of Israel to this day concerning an ounce of the golden calf.

All that is ancient Hebrew history; but, like so much of that history, the golden calf, and the cursed dust of it, all reads to us like a parable and a proverb of our own life. For, what could be said more homecoming and more pungent to all of us than that so many of the cups we drink all our life have so often an ounce of some former sin of ours dropped into them; an ounce of repentance, and of remorse, and of humiliation, and of a broken heart. For an instance in our own Israel: we see Samuel Rutherford, the saintliest of men, going out to a clear spring on the morning of his marriage day and taking a tankardful of the sweet water and dropping into it with his own hands an ounce of his student days in Edinburgh, and drinking the tankard to the dregs before he ventured to take his bride by the hand. And not sensuality only, as in Aaron's case, and in something of that same kind in Samuel Rutherford's case, but all along the line of our sins and faults of youth, an ounce of their accursed dust not seldom comes down and poisons all our enjoyments. Indeed, "poisons all our enjoyments" are Rutherford's very words in a letter of his to Jean Brown, the mother of the famous minister of Wamphray. There had been some sin of Samuel Rutherford's student days, or some stumble sufficiently of the nature of sin, to secretly poison the whole of his subsequent life. Sin is such an essentially poisonous thing that even an almost invisible drop of it let fall into the well-head of a man's life will sometimes absolutely poison the whole deep and broad stream of his after life, as well as all the houses and fields and gardens that are watered out of it. And though God turned the once poisoned waters of the Covenanter's life into very wine and milk, yet to Rutherford's spiritually subtle and detective taste there was always a certain tang of the accursed thing in every sweetest cup of his. And there can be but few men and women among us who have not some Aaron-like, some Rutherford-like, memories behind them that overcloud their most sheltered life and secretly poison their most peaceful conscience. If not a memory of actual sensuality like Aaron's, then a memory of some disingenuity, some simulation or dissimulation of affection, some downright or constructive dishonesty of affection, some lack towards someone of open and entire integrity, some breach of good faith in spirit if not in letter, some still stinging trespass of the golden rule, some horn or hoof of the golden calf, the bitter dust of which they taste in their sweetest cup to the day of their death. There are more men and women among us than anyone would believe who sing their Psalm of David every day with a broken heart—He hath not dealt with us after our sins, nor rewarded us according to our iniquities. As far as the east is from the west, so far hath He removed our transgressions from us.

" An ounce of our past sin and present sinfulness,"

says Rutherford, "becomes a source of sound mortification and humble walking." And his own whole humble life was the best possible proof of that. And so it is with ourselves. Our own past life and our present sinfulness will remain to the end a sure source of spiritual contrition and humble walk before God and man. And how blessed it is that things are ordered so for us! David's Psalms in Holy Scripture, and Rutherford's letters in spiritual literature, rightly read, are full of this experience. O my brethren, what a blessed economy we live under; or, rather, what an ever blessed God is our God who, when Israel was at her worst, revealed Himself at His best! As Paul, with his constant ounce of past sin and present sinfulness, says: "Where sin abounded grace did much more abound."

On one sad occasion in his life William Law felt himself to be debarred from the Lord's Table because of his sin, and at home he occupied the time of the Table in composing a prayer of "deep humiliation," which was found among his secret papers after his death. Like Goodwin, Law spent the time of the Table in taking a turn up and down among the sins of his youth. He revisited all the people on whom he had left the fatal marks of the heels of his feet. He called to mind all those people to whom he had done a hurt he could never heal; all those people whom from youth he had poisoned by word or look or deed; all those people with whose hearts he had recklessly sported; all those people whose homes he had clouded and wrecked; all

AN OUNCE OF THE GOLDEN CALF 143

those people whose hearts he had broken beyond his power ever to bind up. Goodwin took a turn up and down among all such people, rising early every Sabbath morning to do it, before he entered his pulpit to preach Christ and His Cross for sin, as Law did all that banished Communion Day. And after a day of such self-review and self-remorse Law composed at even "a prayer of deep humiliation." I will give you some ounces out of that prayer. "I will arise and go to my Father, and will say, Behold me here, a poor, miserable sinner, weary of myself, and yet unable of myself to return to Thee. Look on an unhappy wretch, full of great guilt, and justly denied any share of this day's blessings. God be merciful to me, who am such a sinner this day that I dare not plead the only atonement for sin. O cut me not off in the midst of my sins, even though I am an unclean worm, a dead dog, a stinking carcase justly cast out from the society of Thy saints. Cast me not away utterly. Despise not utterly the sacrifice of a broken and a contrite heart. O let me never see another such a day as this. Let me never again be so oppressed with guilt and fear and shame as to have to run away from Thy presence and from the fellowship of Thy children. Lord, if Thou wilt, Thou canst make me clean. Wash Thou me, and I shall even yet be whiter than the snow." And always for those whose eyes he had filled with tears he prayed that God would wipe all their tears from off their eyes. His own tears, indeed, from off his own eyes, but theirs especially whose tears he had so unpardonably caused to be shed. And then he would always wind up with that name which God gave to Moses and Aaron and Miriam and to all the elders and to all the people of Israel immediately after the terrible fall of the golden calf: " The Lord, the Lord God, merciful and gracious, long suffering, and abundant in goodness and truth, forgiving iniquity, transgression and sin." And Moses made haste and bowed his head toward the earth and worshipped. But, still, both he and all his people drank all their days each their own ounce of the golden calf.

XVII

SQUEEZING OIL OUT OF A FLINT

IN his classical book on Sanctification Walter Marshall tells his readers that he had been labouring all his days to squeeze oil out of a flint. That is to say, he had been labouring all his days to squeeze holiness out of his own sinful heart. And he had gone on performing that fruitless toil till a great spiritual teacher took him and told him that he was to have all his sanctification, as well as all his justification, out of Jesus Christ alone. That great spiritual teacher tells us that he himself for nearly seven years sought for satisfactory signs of grace in his own heart. It took him all that time till he was taken off entirely from searching for the grounds of peace and the source of power within himself, and was led to look simply to the grace of God and thus to live and grow by faith in Christ alone. Up to that epoch-making conversation with Thomas Goodwin, Walter Marshall's whole life had been one long and painful and fruitless endeavour after inward holiness of mind and heart. But when he opened his whole mind and heart about that matter to Thomas Goodwin, that great spiritual teacher told him that he was to look to Jesus Christ for the sanctifying of his sinful heart, as well as for the cleansing of his sinful conscience. And ever after that illuminating and enfranchising interview with the great Puritan, Marshall set himself to study the person and the work of Christ in a new way, and to preach the person and work of Christ in a new way, till he attained to that eminent spirituality of mind and heart and doctrine out of all which he wrote in his ripe old age his standard work on " The Gospel Mystery of Sanctification."

I will give you in a few words the sum and substance of that spiritual masterpiece. We receive all our holiness of heart, as well as all our peace of conscience, out of Christ's fulness of both these things. Our holiness of heart is a thing already prepared for us and laid up for us in Christ. And thus, even as we are justified by a righteousness that is first wrought out for us by Christ, and which is, from Christ, imputed to us; even so, we are sanctified by a holiness that is first prepared for us in Christ, and is, then, imparted to us out of Christ's fulness. Every atom of our soul-sanctifying holiness is as truly, and as wholly, derived from Christ, as is every atom of our conscience-justifying righteousness. Many serious-minded men, says Marshall, make the greatest of mistakes here; just as he himself made this same greatest of mistakes at one time of his religious life. Many serious-minded men take an infinitude of pains to produce a true holiness for themselves out of their own corrupt hearts; squeezing, all the time, oil out of a flint.

Whereas, the true way, and the only possible way for them to get the mastery over their indwelling sin is by receiving into their hearts a new spiritual nature out of the fulness of that new spiritual nature that is in Christ. And this great truth of the Gospel, says Marshall, if such men but knew it, accepted it and practised it, would save them many an awful hour of heart-agony, and would usher them into a new life of Gospel peace, Gospel holiness, and all manner of Gospel fruitfulness. " Without Me ye can do nothing"—these true words of our Lord stand written on every page of our past life as well as on every page of New Testament Scripture. But with all that, it needs something like a second conversion; it needs something like a second birth from above, to teach us the full blessedness of that great truth, and to deliver us from that great bondage to our inward sinfulness which is so fatal to true holiness of heart and life.

Come, then, since all that is so; come, my brethren, and let us lift up our eyes continually to the Father's Great Olive Tree out of which all the oils of the Holy Spirit pour down into every believing and uplifted heart. For by the ever-adorable Incarnation, and Atonement, and Ascension of His Divine Son, Almighty God has, in Him, created a Second Adam, out of whom we are to draw the whole of our spiritual and eternal life, just as we draw the whole of our natural and temporal life out of the First Adam. And Almighty God has thus, this time, absolutely secured beyond any possibility of shipwreck, the everlasting spirituality, holiness, and blessedness of all those who are truly united to Christ, and are found in Him. And all that is so in order that we who have hitherto to our terrible cost borne the image of the earthly may henceforth bear the image of the heavenly; and that in holiness here and in blessedness hereafter. And it is all this that makes it possible for Jesus Christ to stand forth among us sinful men and to say to us : " I am the True Vine, and My Father is the Husbandman. Abide in Me, and I in you. For without Me ye can do nothing." And it is all this that enables us to teach and to admonish one another in such a spiritual song as this :—

> O loving wisdom of our God !
> When all was sin and shame,
> A Second Adam to the fight
> And to the rescue came.
>
> O wisest love ! that flesh and blood
> Which did in Adam fail,
> Should strive again against the foe,
> Should strive and should prevail.
>
> And that a higher Gift than Grace
> Should flesh and blood refine—
> God's Presence and His very Self
> And Essence all Divine.

Now, since all that is so, let us open Paul, that so Spirit-taught and so eminent saint, and look at some of the droppings of the holy oil that he drew out of Christ ; first, for his own sanctification, and then for the fulness of that so sanctifying Gospel that he was raised up to preach to us. Look at these rich droppings of the Great Olive Tree into

Paul's heart and into his Gospel as he goes over them in this great passage to the Galatians: " Love, joy, peace, long-suffering, gentleness, goodness, faith, meekness, temperance," all of which are the fruits of the Holy Spirit which He produced first in Christ, and which are then out of Christ reproduced in Paul, and in all Paul-like believers to their spiritual sanctification, and to the glory of God.

And, first, take love: that essential oil of the Holy Spirit; that holy oil which God poured out upon Jesus Christ Himself, absolutely without measure; but, all the time, with the view of our receiving of the same holy oil out of Christ, and as He in His sovereignty and grace measures out that oil to us. All up and down his autobiographic Epistles Paul tells his readers that he also had been labouring all his self-righteous days in squeezing oil out of a flint till God took him and revealed His Son in him. After which epoch-making revelation to Paul all his great Epistles are full of Paul's emptiness and of Christ's fulness. Now, I warrant you that it has been the very same with some of yourselves. Some of yourselves have been labouring to squeeze love to God and to your neighbour: a pure, holy, self-forgetting, self-sacrificing love out of a heart that has hitherto yielded you nothing even under the greatest pressure—nothing but the most abominable self-love, self-seeking, self-pleasing, and self-advancing over all other men. Let any man among you watch the workings of his own evil heart for a single day, and see. Just begin to try to love your neighbour as yourself, in this thing and in that, and see. You think that you can easily fulfil that divinest of all the commandments till you once begin to try to do it toward this man and that. But after you have been squeezing at your selfish heart for a lifetime, I hear you—God hears you—crying out in your great agony, "Oh, the wretchedest of all men that I am!" Till one day the Holy Ghost discovers this blessed scripture to you, and writes it with His own finger on your broken heart; this blessed scripture, that without Christ you can do nothing; but that, with Christ, and with enough of Christ, you can do all things. And, henceforth, among all the blessed sayings of your Saviour to you there are none more welcome, and none more meditated on than just that text and its context which runs thus: "As My Father hath loved Me, so have I loved you; continue you in My love. This is My commandment that you love one another as I have loved you. These things I command you, that you love one another." But all that is always to be taken along with this: "Without Me you can do nothing. Abide, therefore, in Me, and I in you."

"Love and joy," writes Paul. And, again, he writes: "Rejoice, evermore." And, again: "Rejoice in the Lord alway, and again I say rejoice." But as we read that in our own so joyless lives we are tempted to turn upon the Apostle and to say to him that if he knew all our sad lot he would not write to us in such an always buoyant strain as that. But before we shut our ears against the Apostle's joyful counsels let us look for a moment at some of his own sorrows, and at how he overcame them.

We cannot suppose that the Apostle is deliberately exaggerating his sorrows, or is telling any untruth about them, when he writes in this way about them: " In much patience, in afflictions, in necessities, in distresses, in stripes, in imprisonments, in tumults, in labours, in watchings, in hunger and in thirst." And again: " In stripes above measure, in prisons more frequent, in deaths oft," and so on, through a catalogue of sufferings only second to those of the Man of Sorrows Himself. Now, is it indeed that same pen which writes to us " to rejoice evermore"? Yes, my brethren, and more than that, the very same pen that writes the most terrible chapter that ever was written by any pen, the seventh of the Romans; that very same pen passes on immediately to write the most joyful chapter that ever was written by any pen, the eighth of the Romans. But then this is the whole explanation of these contradictions and contrasts, this greatly overlooked clause, " Rejoice in the Lord always." For it is in his Lord, and it is in his Lord alone, that Paul has, always, all his joy. Paul puts himself and all his sorrows of all kinds into one scale, and then he puts Christ and all His consolations into another scale, and immediately his light afflictions, which are but for a moment, work for him a far more exceeding and eternal weight of glory. Without Christ and His consolations, Paul had not one atom of true joy; but with Christ in it Paul's cup of consolations ran over. As our cup also will run over, when we put Christ, and all His consolations, into our cup.

"Love, joy, peace." But, here again, when we are urged to the exercise of a constant peace, our restless hearts answer, "Peace, perfect peace? do you say? in this dark world of sin! peace, perfect peace? do you say? with sorrows surging round! peace, perfect peace? our future all unknown? peace, perfect peace? death shadowing us and ours!" Yes! Paul boldly answers to Bickersteth's long string of complaints. Yes, he triumphantly answers, "The peace of God, which passeth all understanding, shall keep your hearts and minds through Christ Jesus." Yes, through Jesus Christ! Grant Christ Jesus, and, though the peace of God will always pass all your understanding, grant Christ Jesus, I say, and the peace of God will no longer pass your experience and your possession.

"Love, joy, peace, long-suffering." Now, says Paul, if we have a true love in our hearts, then we will suffer long with all men, and will, all the time, be kind to them. Only get a few drops daily into your hearts of that oil of love of which Christ's heart is full, and thus all hatred, and all strife, and all resentment, and all impatience will be more and more expelled out of your hearts. And so shall all men know that Christ is the True Vine, and that you are a true branch of the True Vine. Only, again, without Him, I would like to see you trying to live a life of long-suffering, and all the time a life of kindness. Yes, I would like to see the oil of long-suffering that you will squeeze out of a flint!

"Love, joy, peace, long-suffering, and lastly, gentleness." "Gentle Jesus, meek and mild," we teach our children to sing; and we show them in Him and in ourselves, if so be, some examples and some illustrations of His gentleness and ours; some examples for them to imitate both now and when they are no longer children. No doubt Jesus' mother was a perfect gentlewoman. But, all the same, her first-born Son did not draw His incomparable gentleness from His gentle mother. He drew all His incomparable gentleness, directly and immediately, out of the gentleness of the Holy Spirit who so sanctified both the mother and the Son. Go, then, to the same source of all true gentleness, all you who know yourselves to be rude, and rough, and unkind, and ungentle men by nature; go and have yourselves grafted, and grafted ever more and more deeply, into the True Vine, so as to receive out of His fulness a new nature; a copy and an extract and an infusion of His own gentle nature. And so shall all men who know you be compelled to confess out of what an ancient, and honourable, high-bred family you are descended. And the Head of that family will say concerning you also: The same is my sister, and brother, and mother.

Now, as I began with the mention of a masterly book on Gospel Sanctification, written by a master of Israel, I will conclude with a pointed reference to that same book. The congregation will not have forgotten dear old James Stewart of the cab office at the Dean Bridge, who was wont to sit in the front seat down there with all his eyes and all his ears always open to the pulpit and to the desk. Well, at the last pastoral visit I had the privilege of paying to James Stewart's deathbed, laying his hand on Marshall's book, he said: " O ! that Blessed Third Direction ! " And he kissed the old brown book after his own passionate manner and said again: " O ! that heavenly Direction on the Mystical Union ! " Now, if your interest in this matter survives till to-morrow morning, your bookseller will supply you with " Walter Marshall," edited by Andrew Murray of South Africa, and published by Messrs Nisbet at a shilling. Well, then, all you people of sufficient interest and of sufficient enterprise in the life of Sanctification; all you who are old enough and deep enough in the Divine life, be sure to buy and to read and to read again and again, that true classic of the soul. And send it to some of your most intimate friends as a Christmas gift. To all them who are of sufficient intellect and of sufficient heart to appreciate such a great book and especially " The Third Direction." And, if you do so, I warrant you they will thank and bless you all their days for so remembering them and for so honouring them and for so enriching them.

XVIII

JUDAS HEARD ALL JESUS' SERMONS

NOW, if Judas heard his Master's first sermon it could not have failed to make a deep impression upon him. For the text of that so beautiful sermon runs thus to this day, "And He came to Nazareth, where He had been brought up; and, as His custom was, He went into the synagogue on the Sabbath day, and stood up for to read. And there was delivered to Him the Book of the Prophet Esaias. And when He had opened the Book, He found the place where it was written: The Spirit of the Lord God is upon me, because He hath anointed me to preach the Gospel to the poor; He hath sent me to heal the brokenhearted; and to preach deliverance to the captives; and recovering of sight to the blind; and to set at liberty them that are bruised." Now Judas could not fail surely to wonder at the gracious words that proceeded out of his new Master's mouth. And on the spot he must surely have blessed God for the day that made him the chosen disciple of such a Master, and the close follower of such a Saviour sent from God.

At any rate Judas was one of that memorable supper party at which Jesus' enemies cast it in the teeth of the twelve that their Master ate and drank with publicans and sinners. And Judas, to the day of his death, could never surely forget His Master's great reply to that stupid gibe of the Pharisees—this great reply: "They that be whole have no need of a physician, but they that are sick. I came not to call the righteous, but sinners to repentance." Why did Judas not call these divine words to mind before he went out and hanged himself? But by that time Satan had so entered into the traitor's heart that all repentance and all faith and all hope were for ever hidden from his eyes.

Judas was a guest at that other supper party also where the woman who was a sinner washed Jesus' feet with her tears, and did wipe them with the hairs of her head, and kissed His feet, and anointed them with the alabaster ointment. But all that only made Judas the more count up the cost of the ointment and exclaim against its being so shamefully wasted. He heard the "come unto Me" sermon also, and the "bruised reed" sermon and the "prodigal son" sermon, and the "wedding garment" sermon; and, indeed, all his Master's sermons, both of mercy and of judgment.

Look at Judas as he sits under the parable of the sower also, to which parable the Preacher added this: "When any one heareth the word of the kingdom, and understandeth it not, then cometh the wicked one, and catcheth away that which was sown in his heart." He was present at the parable of the tares also, which an enemy had sown among the husbandman's otherwise good wheat. And when Jesus said to the twelve, Have ye understood all these things? Judas no doubt nodded his head in assent like the rest. And so on through the whole of his Master's ministry. Till, at the end of it all, Judas was present in the upper room, and had his feet washed without any remonstrance on his part, so far as has been recorded concerning him. Only, "Master, is it I?" he said. "What thou doest, do quickly," his Master answered him. And Judas went out, and it was night.

And thus it was that of the great passover sermon poor Judas heard not one word. For he had gone out to make his final arrangements with the temple police before his Master uttered one word of that last and best sermon of His. "So when Judas was gone out, Jesus said to the eleven, Now is the Son of Man glorified. And a new commandment I give unto you, that ye love one another. By this shall all men know that ye are My disciples, if ye have love one to another. Let not your heart be troubled. I go to prepare a place for you, that where I am there ye may be also." And so on to the end of a sermon and a prayer that must have melted the heart of the son of perdition himself had he been present to hear that sermon and that prayer. But that was not to be. The only remark I am led to make on that last sermon of our Lord's, and on Judas' absence from it, is this. Every preacher has often felt like Jesus that passover night. Every preacher knows by painful experience how dependent he is on the composition of his congregation and on the character of his hearers. Give a preacher a true, a sincere, an understanding, and an in-earnest audience, and you will get from that preacher his very best work. But on the other hand, let a preacher see a stolid-looking, dull-eyed, absent-minded company of people before him, and his mouth will be shut; or, at best, he will only be able to repeat the platitudes that such a people have been accustomed to hear repeated. "Little children," said Jesus to the eleven—as soon as Judas had gone out. And it is just the same with ourselves in our family worship with our little children. If there is any one present, son, or daughter, or domestic, or guest, who is not the same mind with ourselves in our family worship, our exposition and our prayer are stiff and dry and halting and helpless. But let our little sanctuary be filled with the right people, and our family worship is a daily delight to them and to us. "Judas' departure," says Dr Godet, "set Jesus' heart at liberty that passover night." That is to say, the fourteenth, fifteenth, sixteenth, and especially the seventeenth chapters of John's Gospel would have been all but impossible with Judas still sitting in the upper room.

Now, our Lord, you may be sure, had a very heavy heart all through that last sermon of His, as often at any rate as His eye fell on that vacant seat at the supper table. The deceived disciples thought that Judas had gone out to give something to the poor. But Jesus knows what is in us all.

And He was not deceived about the true reason of Judas' departure. "Every branch in Me that beareth not fruit the husbandman taketh away. Abide in Me, and I in you. If a man abide not in Me, he is cast forth as a branch, and is withered." John Bunyan has Judas under the name of one Mr Temporary. And Thomas Goodwin calls Judas "the most eminent temporary that ever was." Now, you all know what a temporary is. At any rate, I have known not a few of them in my time. And I will select one of them as a specimen of many. Not in order that you may try to recognise him, but rather that you may recognise some of his features in yourselves. Look, then, at that young business man. He was born and brought up in a living church in this city. As a young communicant, I remember how he gladdened his minister's heart, and his father's heart, and his mother's heart, and his elder's heart, till they all looked forward to his becoming a pillar of strength and of ornament in the house of his father's God. But a time of temptation came. A time came when Satan sifted that young man as wheat is sifted. A time came when sides had to be taken in a religious, and a moral, and out of all that a political controversy that I remember well. And it so happened that our young business man was a candidate at that moment for a post that would ultimately bring wealth and station and social distinction to the happy holder of that post. But it was conveyed clearly to our candidate that he need not expect to get that envied post if his name still continued to be associated with that church and with that minister of his. It was a dreadful wrench to him, for he had often confessed that he owed his soul to that implicated minister, and his name was written in honour and in hope on that communion roll. But the tempter kept on telling him that there would be splendid compensations for all those merely sentimental losses. Till the step was taken, and the post was purchased, and the price was paid. But to this day if he meets his old minister in the street of an afternoon that temporary always looks the other way. " This is he that heard the word, and anon with joy received it. Yet had he not root in himself, but dured for a while. But when persecution arose because of the word by and by he was offended." But, then, to tell the whole truth, we are all but so many temporaries, to begin with at any rate. We all cool down from our first heat. We all slow down from our first start. We all stand still, or go back from our first love and loyalty. Only, they who are appointed to final perseverance, and thus to eternal life, they are all, in one way or other, recovered and more than recovered to that from which they had fallen. And in this way they prove themselves not to be of them who draw back unto perdition, but of them that believe to the saving of the soul.

And then there was this: Judas would often preach most excellent sermons himself. For there were seasons when Jesus sent out the twelve as so many probationers in order to test and to practise their preaching gifts, and in order to confirm their intellectual and moral and spiritual character. As thus: "He called unto Him the twelve, and began to send them out two by two, and gave them power over unclean spirits. And He said to them, Whosoever shall not receive you, nor hear you, when ye depart thence, shake off the dust under your feet as a testimony against them." And Judas went out and preached that all men everywhere should repent. Alas! alas! that after all his privileges and all his opportunities and all his services, this should be said on the day of Pentecost concerning him: Judas, which was guide to them that took Jesus, was at one time numbered with us, and obtained part of our ministry. Now, this same man purchased a field with the reward of his iniquity, and that field is called the field of blood. Let his habitation be desolate, and his bishoprick let another take. It was the like of this that made the greatest of the apostles to say: "I keep under my body, and bring it into subjection, lest that by any means, after I have preached to others, I myself should be a castaway."

Now, my brethren, all that concerning poor Judas serves to show us that it is not the best preaching we can get that is the one thing needful. The one thing needful is an instant and a persevering obedience to the thing preached. On that matter, listen to the Great Preacher Himself. "Whosoever heareth these sayings of Mine, and doeth them, I will liken him to a wise man which built his house upon a rock. And every man that heareth these sayings of Mine, and doeth them not, shall be likened to a foolish man which built his house upon the sand, and that house fell, and great was the fall of it." Now, if Judas had taken all his household that Sabbath night, and every Sabbath night, and had made them tell him all they remembered of every sermon, and had then rightly divided the word of truth, first to himself, and then to all his family, what a wise man Judas Iscariot would have been, and what a pattern parent! And how we would all have been following out his good example every Sabbath evening, to our own salvation and to the salvation of our children! And, in that happy case, Judas would soon have been a pillar-apostle in the Church of Jerusalem, and his eldest son would have succeeded him in his bishoprick when he entered into his eternal rest. But, as it was, both Judas and his eldest son, being dead, yet speak to us. I think I can make out what they say to me and to my children. Can you make out just what they say to you and to your children?

XIX

THE WORD WHEN IT IS MIXED WITH FAITH

"A JEST'S prosperity," says Shakespeare, "lies in the ear of him that hears it, never in the tongue of him that makes it." And much more is that the case with a sermon. You have to bring a keen sense of wit and humour to hear and to enjoy a good jest aright; but you have to bring a keen sense of your own sinfulness, and a great hunger after holiness, to hear a good sermon aright. To hear a really good sermon, as it ought to be heard, demands almost as much mind and heart; nay, almost as much sweat and tears and blood as it demands to compose it and to preach it. And hence arises the utter unprofitableness of so much of our preaching and of your hearing.

"But how is the word to be read and heard that it may become effectual to salvation?" asks the best of Catechisms. And it supplies this best of answers. "That the word may become effectual to salvation, we must attend thereunto with diligence, preparation, and prayer: receive it with faith and love, lay it up in our hearts and practise it in our lives." Now, every preacher knows in his own conscience whether or no he has composed and preached his sermon with diligence, preparation, and prayer. And every hearer also has his own conscience every Sabbath Day in that same matter. Now, we are told in the context that even when the sermons were of the very best, all the time, the hearers had within them an evil heart of unbelief. That is to say, they had neither faith nor love nor hope wherewith to mix the word. And thus it was that the word preached did not profit them. John Owen points out that there is a *litotes* in the text. That is to say, far less is said literally than we are to understand to be said. It is not that the word preached did not do them any good, but it is this rather, that every sermon they heard did them great harm. It was as Paul himself says about so much of his apostolic preaching; and he says it with the deepest pain and sorrow of heart, that, to not a few of his hearers, every new sermon of his was a savour of death unto death. And Peter also has much the same lament to make about much of his preaching. "Wherefore, laying aside all malice, and all guile, and all hypocrisies, and all envies, and all evil speakings, as new-born babes, desire the sincere milk of the word, that you may grow thereby. Unto you therefore that believe, He is precious; but unto them which be disobedient, He is a stone of stumbling, and a rock of offence, even to them that stumble at the word, being disobedient thereto." Good preaching; preaching like Paul's preaching and Peter's, is no jest to the preacher. But, at the same time, it is by far the best occupation on earth when the hearer mixes every new sermon with new faith and new love and new obedience, and thus secures, both to himself and to the preacher, the present success and the everlasting profit of every new sermon that he hears.

And not the preaching of the word only; but why are the public prayers of the sanctuary so unprofitable to us all? For the very same reason: our public prayers are not mixed aright and enough with faith in them that speak them and in them that hear them spoken. The very first elements of all true prayer have not been learned aright, neither by the occupant of the pulpit nor by the occupant of the pew. He who conducts the prayers of the congregation is much more conscious of the presence and the audience and the opinion of the people than he is of the presence and the audience and the opinion of God. But when the minister is really conscious of the presence of God, then it is that all the people are caught up and carried into the same Presence in spite of themselves. The very first principle of all public prayer, as of all other prayer, is this—that GOD IS, and that He hears and answers all earnest and believing prayer. Well, then, always, as soon as the minister says, Let us pray, that moment say to yourself that God is present to hear the minister and you and to answer him and you. And if you mix faith with your prayer in that way you will go home every Sabbath-day to say, Surely the minister had great power with God to-day; surely God was present to bless us all to-day. While, all the time, all the difference was in yourself. It was the way you mixed every word of his prayer with faith that gave the minister such power, and gave God such an opportunity to hear you and to answer you.

And, then, let it be the same with the public praise. The true grace of praise is the very same as the true grace of prayer. And it begins in praise as in prayer by the faith that GOD IS, and that He inhabits the praises of Israel, and, especially, your praises. Always, therefore, as soon as the praise is again given out, recollect that the choir, and the organ, and all else of that kind, are here not for God's sake, or in any way to please Him or to prevail with Him. God does not need our instruments; no, nor even our voices. All He stipulates for is our hearts. All He asks is that we offer to Him no psalm, nor paraphrase, nor hymn, nor anthem, nor spiritual song till we have well mixed it with repentance, and with faith, and with thanksgiving. And, then, to assist us in that, we are allowed and are encouraged to make use of the very best voices and the very best instruments to stir up somewhat our slow minds, and to kindle up somewhat our cold hearts. Only put yourselves aright into your praises, and both God and His holy angels will descend to hear you sing.

And then, when we go outside the church, the thing nearest the church-preaching and prayer and praise is our family worship. But there is nothing, either in the church or outside of it, that is more

God-forsaken and dreary and wearisome than our so-called family worship. Our public worship is dreary enough and wearisome enough when it is not mixed with immediate and sufficient faith. But in public worship there is always the congregation to interest us, and there is the music, and there is the pulpit oratory, if so be. But, lacking all these attractions, family worship, with most of us, has a dullness and a dreariness that threaten to extinguish the ordinance out of our fatherland altogether. And that, because here again, the whole thing is so wholly without its proper faith either in the performer of the domestic ceremony or in those who are compelled to be present at the recurring ceremonial. With an intelligent and an instructed faith in all concerned, our morning and evening worship of God in our families would soon become as necessary to us, and as welcome to us, as our morning and evening meals. And much more so. Thy word is more to me, said an Old Testament householder, than is my necessary food. But as things are with us many thoughtful and anxious heads of houses are feeling an ever-increasing difficulty in being able to interest, and to instruct, and to impress, and to carry along with them, all their assembled households, and to divide aright, to old and young, their portion of the word of truth. But let all such anxious and burdened men take heart of hope. Things may, all the time, be better with them than they think. "So far as I reckon," writes Thomas Halyburton, "it was about this time that the Lord began to make Himself known to the Lady Ann Elcho: which made her to bless Him on her deathbed for my family worship. And how much I wondered to be told that! For my mistakes and my mismanagements in that exercise had been so many; and the proper mixture of my faith in all parts of it had been so seldom, and so weak at its best."

But even worse than our family worship is the faithless way and the positively indecent way we are wont to say grace at every family meal. When William Law went out to dinner this was the way that grace was wont to be said in his day in England. "In one house you will see the head of the house just pulling off his hat; in another, half getting up from his seat; another shall, it may be, proceed so far as to make as if he said something; we can hardly bear with him that seems to say grace with any degree of seriousness; and we look upon it as a sign of a fanatical temper, if a man has not done as soon as he has begun." We have all seen that to the letter in Scotland, as well as in England; and in our own houses, as well as in the graceless houses to which we have gone out to dine. Indeed, we never see anything else either at home or abroad. Now, if any of you have ever felt the shame and the pain and the mockery of all that, and would like to have it otherwise at your own table, you might begin to show some little life and originality and reality at your family meals, and that in some of these ways. You might vary your graces from day to day, and from meal to meal. You might repeat a well-selected verse of Scripture

THE WORD WHEN MIXED WITH FAITH 169

at one time; and, then, two or three words of your own out of a warm heart, at another time. At one time you might ask some devout-minded guest to sanctify your meal; and at another time get your little boy to say one of his nursery verses or schoolroom texts. And, always, when you say grace yourself give them all a good example. Look upward for a moment above all surrounding persons and things, and say—My table Thou hast furnished, and my cup overflows. And say at another time that you sit down at your full table well remembering Him who had not where to lay His head, and who went out in the morning not knowing where He would sup and sleep that night. And the more you mix every successive dish with a thankful faith like that the more will your meal recruit and refresh you, and the better company you will be to all about you.

And, then, after dining with the Czar this was the way that Father John went to bed, and this was the way that he counselled his people in Cronstadt to go to bed. "Do not forget," he said, "to confess with all sincerity and importunity and contrition all the sins into which you have fallen during the past day. A few moments of prayer, properly mixed with faith, will cleanse you from all your iniquity before you sleep. Often during the day, and often by the indiscretions of the table in eating and drinking and talking, I have been a great transgressor. But after I was again alone for a little with God, I have lain down with the peace of God filling my heart. How needful will it be for our blessed Lord to come to us all with His salvation at the evening of our life, and at the decline of our days! O save me both now and then, and save me wholly, O my most gracious Saviour, and receive me at the end of all my days into Thy heavenly kingdom!" Be sure, my brethren, to mix the end of every day of yours with a faith like that of the Czar's favourite chaplain, now with God.

And, then, if you once begin to mix faith in that way with all your church life, and with all your family life, you will be led on to mix your whole life, at all times, and in all places, with the same all-profiting faith and love and holy obedience. All the successes, all the comforts, all the enjoyments, and all the possessions of your life will be enhanced and enriched, and, indeed, sanctified to you: and that, in the exact measure that you mix them all with faith and love and thankfulness to Him from whom alone all your blessings ever come to you. As, again, when your times of trial and tribulation come to you, your long practice of faith in God will enable you to take all your troubles, immediately and exclusively, from His hand alone. And in this way, as this life goes on, you will attain to such a sure and near and intimate life and walk of faith with God that there will be times when you will not know whether you are in the body or out of the body, God will so satisfy you with His salvation and with Himself. Till this will be your continual psalm to Him: "Nevertheless I am continually with Thee. Thou hast holden me by my right hand. Thou shalt guide me with Thy counsel, and afterward receive me to glory. Whom have I in heaven but Thee? And there is none upon earth that I desire beside Thee. My flesh and my heart often faileth; but God is always the strength of my heart, and He will be my portion for ever."

XX

AN INSTINCT FOR CHRIST

"NO man can come to Me, except the Father which hath sent Me draw him." And Thomas Goodwin, the greatest of all our pulpit expositors, has repeatedly paraphrased these words of our Lord, and has described the Father's work as the implanting in the soul of an instinct for Christ.

But, then, to begin with, what exactly is an instinct? Well, according to the late Sir James Murray, our latest and best authority, an instinct, etymologically and scientifically and experimentally taken, is something that inwardly instigates, incites, and impels a living creature to some outward action. An instinct is an inborn and a powerful impulse toward something beyond itself. And, after his so instructive method, the great lexicographer supplies his students with column after column of historically arranged examples and illustrations of that universal use of the word. Let all those who are happy enough to possess or to have access to the New Oxford Dictionary consult that great work under the entry of "Instinct," and they will there find a great light thrown upon our present text.

As we read the opening chapters of the Book of Genesis we are present at the first implantation of that which is a universal and an omnipotent instinct in all God's creatures that have received their life from Him. And God said, Let the earth bring forth the living creature, each after its kind, cattle and creeping thing, and beast of the earth, each after his own kind, and let them multiply, and replenish the earth, and it was so. Not that we are to suppose that the Creator made a spoken address to the creatures in as many words. No. But in their first creation He put that all-commanding instinct into all His creatures to love one another and so to multiply their kind. And thus it is that we see the summer bees all around us to-day still following out their creation instinct in the way they build up their honeycombs and so industriously replenish them for their young ones. All the birds of the air also by a springtime instinct construct and furnish and provision their nests. The ants are a people not strong, says Solomon, yet they also prepare their meat in the summer. The conies also are a feeble folk; and therefore they make their homes among the rocks. The locusts also have no king, but they go forth all of them by bands. The ox, says Isaiah, instinctively knows his owner, and the ass his master's crib. Yea, says Jeremiah, the stork in the heavens knoweth her appointed time, and the crane and the swallow and the turtle; they all observe the time of their coming.

"An instinct," says Archdeacon Paley in his own clear English, "is a propensity prior to experience, and a propensity which is independent of education." Now, the drawing of the soul to its Saviour is something not unlike all that. The drawing of the Father in the new creature is something not at all unlike the instincts with which He draws all His creatures to their proper objects and their proper ends. That is to say, the Father's drawing is not at all unlike an instinct in its originality, in its spontaneity, in its directness, in its ultimateness, in its exclusiveness, in its unanalyzableness, and in its infallibleness. For, all that, and far more than all that, is contained and is conveyed in these few so filial and so evangelical words of our Blessed Lord: "No man can come to Me, except the Father which hath sent Me draw him. And all that the Father giveth Me shall come to Me; and him that cometh unto Me I will in no wise cast out."

Now, it will for ever ennoble and sanctify and glorify this hitherto humble word to you, if I succeed in my high endeavour to apply this word, in the first place, to our Blessed Lord Himself. Which application I now proceed to make with a thousand Old and New Testament Scriptures to help me in so doing. For, what are these but the utterances and the expressions of a great divine instinct, so to call it, first in the mouth of the promised Messiah, and then in the mouth of the Son of God come in the flesh? Such inspired and such instinctive utterances as these: "Lo, I come, in the volume of the Book it is written of Me, I delight to do Thy will, O my God: yea, Thy law is within my heart." And, again, how inward and how instinctive is this: " The Lord hath called me from the womb; from the bowels of my mother hath He made mention of my name. And He hath made my mouth like a sharp sword: in the shadow of His hand hath He hid me, and made me like a polished shaft; in His quiver hath He hid me." And, again, what an evangelical instinct is here: " The Lord God hath given me the tongue of the learned, that I should know how to speak a word in season to him that is weary." And if this is not the sweetest and surest instinct on earth, glorified up to heaven itself, I do not know what else to call it: " Can a woman forget her sucking child, that she should not have compassion on the son of her womb? Yea, she may forget, yet will I not forget thee." And again: " Yea, I have loved thee with an everlasting love: therefore with loving-kindness have I drawn thee." And, then, after that everlasting love had drawn the Son of God down to this world, the blessed pages of the Four Gospels are simply full to overflowing of that same divine love now inspired and implanted for ever in the human heart of the Man Jesus Christ. So much so, that I will put it to all you who know your New Testament to say: does Thomas Goodwin go one syllable too far when he pursues this great theme in his own exquisite way, and says (I will give you a short selection): " God the Father," he says, " has given Jesus Christ a special injunction to love and to save sinners. And to secure that end He has implanted a gracious instinct, even a divine predisposition and inclination in Christ's heart toward sinners. God the Father has implanted an instinct; an overpowering passion, indeed, in the heart of our Redeemer, such as He implants in all parents for their own children. Yea, God the Father laid this on Christ, that if He would have His Father love Him, then He must be sure, from His heart, and with His whole heart, to love us. So much so, that even now that He is in heaven —nay, rather, much more that He is now in heaven —His holy instinct of love to us boils up in His heart everlastingly. We are apt to think that Christ being now so high, and so holy, and so happy, that, therefore, He will be somewhat sour and sharp toward such sinners as we are. We are often tempted to think so. But the fact is the very opposite. For Christ remains as meek, as lowly minded, as approachable, and as affable in heaven as ever He was on earth. Nay, I will say, much more in heaven. So much so, that to all manner of men, and in all their sin, and in all their aggravation of sin, He bows down, and Himself proclaims; Him that cometh unto Me, I will in no wise cast out, but will save all such to the uttermost. Our young preachers," continues Goodwin, " choose their first texts according to their tempers and feelings and intentions toward their future people. And so this was Christ's first text, and He took to it by a holy instinct: The Spirit of the Lord is upon me, because He hath anointed me to preach the Gospel to the poor. He hath sent me to heal the brokenhearted: to preach deliverance to the captives, and the recovering of sight to the blind, and to set at liberty them that are bruised. And this day is this Scripture fulfilled in your ears."

But, all the same, all that in Christ would be but thrown away unless the Father secured our salvation by implanting a corresponding instinct in our souls for Christ as our Saviour. According to these words of our Lord on this matter: " No man can come to Me, except the Father which hath sent Me draw him." And, already, that divine drawing, and the implanting of that divine instinct, is described in these never-to-be-forgotten words of God in the prophet Ezekiel: " A new heart will I give you, and a new spirit will I put within you, and I will take the stony heart out of your flesh, and I will give you an heart of flesh." And the absolute necessity for the implantation of such a divine instinct in us, and the creation of such a new and spiritual nature in us, is laid down by our Lord Himself in words that can never be watered down or explained away: " Verily, verily, I say unto you, except a man be born again, and born from above, he can neither enter nor ever see the Kingdom of God." And all who have been so born are thus described in the opening of John's so spiritual Gospel: " To those gave He power to become the sons of God: to them which were born, not of blood, nor of the will of man, nor of the will of the flesh, but of God." And, following up that, all the New Testament Epistles have this same truth written all over them as with a sunbeam, as thus: " In Christ Jesus neither circumcision availeth anything, nor

M

uncircumcision, but a new creature." And again: "And you hath He quickened who were dead in trespasses and sins: even when we were dead in sins, He hath quickened us together with Christ." And again: "According to His mercy He saved us by the washing of regeneration and the renewing of the Holy Ghost." And again: "Of His own will begat He us with the word of truth, that we should be a kind of first-fruits of His creatures." And again: "Being born again, not of corruptible seed, but of incorruptible, by the word of God which liveth and abideth for ever." And what could possibly be more of a divinely implanted instinct than this: "Whosoever is born of God does not commit sin, for his seed remaineth in him, and he cannot sin, because he is born of God"? Now, what is all that but an expanding and an enforcing and an applying of our present text, and of Goodwin's paraphrase of our present text: "drawn of the Father, and that by a divinely implanted instinct"?

But to come to some particulars. To take some specialised instincts of our souls for Christ, and for the things of Christ. And let us take first that most pungent and most commanding of all our spiritual instincts; the instinct of a guilty and an awakened conscience for the cleansing and peace-speaking blood of Christ. "As a deer," says Goodwin, "when it is struck with a dart, runs presently to the herb called *dictamnus*, and takes no rest till it finds that healing herb of its Creator that He has had planted for its cure; even so is a conscience-stricken sinner drawn of God to the blood of Christ." Yes, we have all been like that dart-stricken deer ten thousand times. Ten thousand times we have had no rest from our inward wound till that evangelical instinct which God planted in us had so commandingly drawn us to the Cross of Christ, and through the Cross of Christ to that peace of conscience which passes all understanding.

And again: a thousand times you must all have felt a like instinct drawing you to the throne of grace. You will be sitting alone, or you will be walking abroad alone, and in the multitude of your thoughts within you a secret Hand will take hold of your heartstrings and will powerfully draw you to the mercy seat. It is the Father. It is the text. It is an instinct of the Holy Ghost. And as you yield yourself up to its drawing and impelling, a great enlargement, a great liberty, a great peace, and a great power with God suddenly fill your whole soul. Thomas Shepard said that he was sometimes so full of sin and its estranging wages that he would rather die than go to his knees and abide on his knees before God. While at other times such an instinct for prayer would take possession of him that he could continue to pray without ceasing. And the great pilgrim father could find no other explanation of that mysterious experience but the explanation offered by Christ: No man can come to Me, except the Father which hath sent Me draw him.

And so again with your books about Christ. This very afternoon a score of books will lie on your

Sabbath-day table. But, instinctively, you will set them all aside but one. Instinctively, you will be drawn to take up one special book. And you will spend an hour, two hours, three hours on a book that at one time you would not have opened though you had been paid to do it. Now, what is it that has made you so to differ this afternoon? There is only one possible answer to that question. The Father has drawn you to His Son, and thus to that book about His Son. All your other books are good for other days and for other purposes. But this is now to you the day that God hath made for His Son, and for the literature concerning His Son, and concerning His Son's work for you and in you. A literature compared with which all other literature is ephemeral and superficial and wholly unworthy of the Lord's Day, and of your everlasting interest in Him and in the day of His death and of His resurrection for you. And God's own hand has had that book written and laid on your table for you, and for all in your household like you. And by a divinely implanted instinct you are now guided spontaneously, sweetly, infallibly, to the right literature for you.

And, speaking of the Sabbath, and of an instinct for the Sabbath, some of you will think it preposterous and impossible in Wordsworth to say a thing like this about two schoolboys, but I assure you that the great poet has written every word of this and I know it to be true :—

"And once I said,
As I remember, looking round upon these rocks

> And hills, on which we all of us were born, I
> Said that God, who made the great book of the world,
> Would bless such piety,—
> Never did worthier lads break English bread,—
> The finest Sunday that the autumn saw,
> With all its mealy clusters of ripe nuts,
> Never could keep those boys away from church,
> Or tempt them to one hour of Sabbath breach,
> Leonard and James.

Now, all that: the blood of Christ; the throne of grace; the books about Christ; the Day of Christ; and all the rest that belongs to Christ—all that in some men's souls, like an accumulated instinct, like a manifold cord of God, draws them spontaneously, irresistibly, unerringly, and infallibly to Christ and to their everlasting salvation through Christ. And that, because the Father is in all these things drawing those men through Christ to Himself. Now, yes or no: would any of you fain have an instinct like that, and to issues like these, implanted in your soul? Well, then, the text is written to tell what you have to do in order to secure to yourself that supreme blessing, that all-comprehending and everlasting blessing. And this text, taken down from Christ's own lips, tells you plain as plain can be, Who it is alone that can do all that in you and for you. "No man cometh unto Me, except the Father which hath sent Me draw him. And all that the Father giveth Me shall come to Me, and him that cometh to Me I will in no wise cast out." O Lamb of God, I come. Just as I am, I come.

XXI

CONSENT MAKES THE MATCH

A SWEETER chapter was never written than the twenty-fourth of Genesis. The beautiful domestic picture of aged Abraham swearing his most trusty servant concerning a suitable bride for Isaac, his well-beloved son; that trusty servant's prayerful journey to Padanaram; the maiden Rebekah at the well with her pitcher; and then her frank consent; this love-inspired chapter is a perfect gem of ancient eastern authorship. And they said, We will call the damsel, and enquire at her mouth. And they called Rebekah, and said unto her, Wilt thou go with this man? And she she said, I will go. And they sent away Rebekah their sister, and her nurse, and Abraham's servant, and his men. And they blessed Rebekah, and said unto her, Thou art our sister, be thou the mother of thousands of millions, and let thy seed possess the gate of those which hate them. And she said, I will go.

Though no one knew it, and though she did not know it herself, her heart had been Isaac's all the time. The oft-told family story of Abraham's call;

his son Isaac's fair and princely youth; and then more than all that, his being offered by his father on the altar on Mount Moriah, and his miraculous deliverance by the angel of God—all that had for long been a household word in Rebekah's mother's house, and all that from her childhood up had fired Rebekah's young and tender heart. And thus it was that day after day as she went out to her father's well for water she looked away west over the vast sands of Mesopotamia and wished that it had been God's will that she had been born a man-child, so that she too might have been chosen and called of God to go out to His land of promise and there to have had her part in founding an elect family of saints and princes and great servants of God. And now what is this that God hath wrought for His handmaiden? Is she not beside herself? Is not this all a day-dream? Till her heart bounds up to her father's God and blesses Him as she waters camel after camel, the very camels that are Abraham's and Isaac's camels. And never did woman's heart go out of a woman's bosom as did Rebekah's heart when Abraham's servant put Isaac's earrings of gold upon her ears and his bracelets of gold upon her arms. Had Rebekah had to walk barefoot over all the burning sands that lay between her father's house and the Land of Promise, nothing would have kept Rebekah back from an election and a call so divine and so sweet as was that so warm and so urgent argument of Eliezer the servant of Abraham and Isaac. Hearken, O daughter, and consider, and incline thine ear; forget also thine own people and thy father's house. Yes, or ever I was aware, says the bride in the song, my heart made me like the chariots of Amminadib. And so Rebekah said, Yes, I will go!

"It is consent that makes the match," says Thomas Goodwin on the text. Yes, so it is. And so it was with the match between Isaac and Rebekah. It was not Abraham's faith and foresight that made that match. Nor was it his great wealth. Nor was it Isaac's princely presents of gold and silver. Nor was it Eliezer's passionate pleadings. No; nor all these things taken together. It was Rebekah's own consent, that alone made that match. It was when she said, Yes, I will go! From that moment that match was made. And so it is with the match between the Lord Jesus Christ and the believing soul; that heavenly match for the sake of which all this chapter and every chapter is written. It is not the Father's eternal election and predestination that make the match. It is not even that the eternal Son of God has loved the soul with an everlasting love. It is not even that He is fairer than the children of men. It is not even the heart-captivating story of Mount Calvary. Nor is it all the heart-impressing Gospel pleading of all the best friends of the Bridegroom. No; it is the soul's own consent; the soul's own unconstrained and spontaneous consent; that, and that alone, makes the match. All else is beside the mark.

Now, my fellow-believers, it would be something like that—was it not?—when you first gave the Son of God your consent. You had heard Jesus Christ preached from your youth up. You had sat and listened to the enthralling story of the Cross of Christ at communion seasons and on Easter Sabbaths. You had sometimes wished that He would come Himself and carry your heart captive for ever to Himself. But it always seemed to you as if you were to be passed by, and that you were to spend all your days in your great desolation of heart. Till, as God would have it, a wonderful dispensation of Divine grace came to you one Sabbath-day—a Sabbath-day never to be forgotten by you. For on that day, as never before, Jesus Christ was preached to you: to you, as it seemed to you, chosen out of the whole congregation, and so both Christ Himself and His whole salvation were pressed upon you by that friend of the Bridegroom that, ere ever you were aware, your heart was in a flame of love, like the heart of the bride in the Song. And ever since that espousal day in your secret heart you have been Christ's, and He has been yours.

Not, indeed, that the marriage of the Lamb has even yet altogether come. No. But all the time, and till it comes, He is preparing a place for you, and you are making yourself ready for Him. As the word is, you are engaged to be married, one day, to the Son of God. And you have His sure word for it that He will come again, and will receive you to Himself, that where He is there you may be also. Even so, come quickly, Lord Jesus! This ring of Thine upon my hand is good, but it only makes my heart burn the more till Thy left arm is under my head. and till Thy right arm embraces me. Yes, the Communion table is good, but, O my soul, what will it be when He shall take thee into His banqueting house, and when His banner over thee shall be love! " And I John saw the holy city, new Jerusalem, coming down from God out of Heaven, prepared as a bride adorned for her husband. And I heard a great voice out of Heaven saying, Behold, the tabernacle of God is with men, and He will dwell with them, and they shall be His people, and God Himself shall be with them, and be their God. And God shall wipe away all tears from their eyes; and there shall be no more death, neither sorrow, nor crying, neither shall there be any more pain; for the former things are passed away." And they said, We will call the damsel, and enquire at her mouth. And they called Rebekah, and said unto her, Wilt thou go with this man? And she said, I will go.

But, O most happily! consent makes the match oftener than once. For, even when the original match has been dishonoured and destroyed, the same consent renewed will restore the match and will make it better than ever before. Not to speak of the Book of Genesis, did you ever read the Book of the Prophet Hosea? If you have ever really read that terrible book you will agree with me that it was not written for babes at the breast. Such strong meat as that belongeth only to them that are of full age: even to those who by reason of use have their senses exercised in spiritual things. After the more-than-earthly sweetness of the Song of Solomon, and after the surpassing loving-kindness of Isaiah, we positively shudder with shame and with terror and with horror when we open that awful Book of Hosea. But we shudder with far more shame and terror and horror—some of us—when we come here to-day to confess a far more terrible unfaithfulness in our own souls. For Jesus Christ the Son of God is our Hosea the son of Beeri, and our own souls are Gomer the daughter of Diblaim, with her three children, Jezreel, and Lo-ruhamah, and Loammi. But as we read on we come to see to our great amazement that the Book of Hosea is not a bill of divorcement as we fully expected it would be: nor does it contain the name of any of Hosea's creditors to whom he had sold Gomer and her children. But as we read on, to our utter amazement we come on this heart-breaking and heart-compelling exhortation: " O Israel, return unto the Lord thy God ; for thou hast fallen by thine iniquity. Take with you words, and turn to the Lord: say unto Him, Take away all iniquity, and receive us graciously: for in Thee the unfaithful wife and the fatherless children findeth mercy. I will heal their backsliding, I will love them freely: for Mine anger is turned away. I will be as the dew unto Israel: he shall grow as the lily, and cast forth his roots as Lebanon. Behold I will allure her into the wilderness and will speak comfortably to her. And I will give her her vineyards from thence, and the valley of Achor for a door of hope : and she shall sing there, as in the days of her youth, and of her first espousals. And I will betroth thee to Me again, and for ever : yea, I will betroth thee unto Me in righteousness, and in loving-kindness, and in tender mercies. I will even betroth thee unto Me in faithfulness: and thou shalt know the Lord." And then, after that, there comes in this greater than ever, this better than ever, marriage song. You all have that epithalamium song by heart. But I will repeat it to you to re-awaken it within your heart :—

> Come, let us to the Lord our God
>   With contrite hearts return ;
> Our God is gracious, nor will leave
>   The desolate to mourn.
>
> Our hearts, if God we seek to know,
>   Shall know Him, and rejoice ;
> His coming like the morn shall be,
>   Like morning songs His voice.
>
> So shall His presence bless our souls,
>   And shed a joyful light ;
> That hallowed morn shall chase away
>   The sorrows of the night.

Well, then, O greatly backsliding communicants, your re-engagement to your heavenly Husband is to be but a better repetition of your first engagement. And now, as then, consent always makes the match. Only give your consent to return, and all will be forgiven and forgotten at the Table to-day.

> Hark! my soul! it is the Lord;
> 'Tis thy Saviour, hear His word;
> Jesus speaks, and speaks to thee,
> "Say, poor sinner, lov'st thou Me?"
>
> I delivered thee when bound,
> And, when bleeding, healed thy wound;
> Sought thee wandering, set thee right;
> Turned thy darkness into light!
>
> Mine is an unchanging love,
> Higher than the heights above,
> Deeper than the depths beneath,
> Free and faithful, strong as death.

"Say, poor sinner, lov'st thou Me?" Your own broken heart will give Him your answer. Just think of all that has come and gone between Christ and you—just think who but Christ would ever speak to you again after all that has come and gone? Who but Christ would take you to His heart again, and all without bitterness or upbraiding? Who but He would engage to make you whiter than snow, and to present you, without spot or blemish, before the Father in love? But you say that you are such an unworthy communicant! Yes, indeed; so you are. But what was Gomer the daughter of Diblaim? And yet, with all her terrible unfaithfulness to her husband, it was simply her consent to return to him that made his broken heart so glad. Her consent to return made that broken-hearted man to rejoice over her more than any other bridegroom in all Israel ever rejoiced over his pure and unspotted bride. That supernatural return and reconciliation recorded in that wonderful book was only made possible because Hosea was an evangelical prophet; and as such, personified and anticipated Jesus Christ in His renewed reception of backsliding believers. All this, you must understand, was first enacted in Hosea's house, and was then written in his great Gospel book, not for Hosea's and Gomer's sake, it was all enacted and written that it might be read and repeated and re-enacted in this house this day. Only consent to return to Christ this day, and your story will as far eclipse the story of Hosea and Gomer as the heaven eclipses the earth. Only consent where you sit and thou shalt no more be termed forsaken, neither shall thy land any more be termed desolate. But thou shalt be called Hephzibah, and thy land Beulah; for thy Lord still delighteth in thee, and thy land shall be married. And Eliezer, Abraham's servant, brought forth jewels of silver and jewels of gold, and gave them to Rebekah. He gave also to her brother and to her mother precious things. And they did eat and drink, he and the men that were with him, and tarried all night. And they rose up early in the morning, and he said, Send me away to my master. And her brother and her mother said, Let the damsel abide with us a few days, at the least ten, and after that she shall go. And the servant said to them, Hinder me not, seeing the Lord hath prospered my way; but send me away that I may go to my master. And they said, We will call the damsel, and will enquire at her mouth. And they called Rebekah, and said unto her, Wilt thou go with this man? And she said, I will go. And her consent made the match.

XXII

THE PRACTICE OF THE PRESENCE OF CHRIST

"THE Practice of the Presence of God," by Brother Lawrence, is a Catholic classic of rare intellectual excellence and of great spiritual value. I have known the exquisite little gem from my student days and I have often received great spiritual benefit from the prayerful perusal of it. But the longer I live and the older I grow the more I have come to feel that the little Catholic classic is far too little evangelical for me. Indeed, it is far too little Christian for me. St. Augustine would not have found the Name of Jesus Christ enough in it for him. And I have become somewhat like St. Augustine myself in that same respect. Profoundly spiritual and fruitfully devotional as Lawrence's little masterpiece always is to me, at the same time as often as I open it nowadays I straightway begin to draw out an improved and an enriched and an evangelical edition of it for myself. And in this way. From the title-page onwards through all the Conversations and Letters of the little book I always read my private copy of Lawrence in this amended manner: "The Practice of the Presence of God, *as God is in Christ.*" And it is only when I do so that I enter into the full riches of this so enriching little book. And thus I am able to make it another help to the fuller and ever fuller appreciation of my supreme blessedness in the Word having been made flesh for me. All that Brother Lawrence says so powerfully and so impressively about the practice of the presence of GOD is only fully true to me when I read into it the Person and the Presence of JESUS CHRIST THE SON OF GOD. And I feel sure that had the Carmelite brother but sat at the feet of the Great Reformer his little book would have been far more scripturally and far more evangelically written than it is. That is to say, Jesus Christ would then have had His true and His proper place in Lawrence's little classic. And that on the Christological and apostolical and evangelical and experimental principle that all men must honour the Son even as they honour the Father. And on the principle of this Divine Commandment also: Ye believe in God; believe also in Me.

I have alluded to Luther in this connection, but not at all with a controversial intention. Not at all. But only for the sake of the truth as the truth is in Jesus. For the sake of that truth which, among others, was so conspicuously committed to Luther's charge, and which was so richly proclaimed to the modern world in his incomparable preaching. Luther handles the Divine Nature of Jesus Christ, and the blessedness of the practice of the Presence of Jesus Christ, with a power and with an impressiveness all his own. Take these so eminently Christian passages of his out of a thousand such: "True Christian divinity," he says, "setteth not God forth in His absolute Divine Majesty. True Christian divinity commands us not to attempt to search out the unsearchable Godhead, but to know God as He has revealed Himself in His Incarnate Son." Again: "The Christian religion begins, not at the Highest, as other religions begin, but at the Lowest. Run, therefore, and begin at the manger and embrace that Infant of days who lies swaddled there for thee. Behold Him as He was born for thee, as He was brought up, as He went about doing good, as He died on the cross, as He rose again, as He ascended up above all heavens, and as He has now absolute power over all men and all things: and all for thee." Again: "Since we can never comprehend the Eternal, for this cause the Eternal Himself said, I will send to them My Son in their own flesh, in order that through Him they may somewhat know Me." And again: "All the wisdom of this world," says Luther, "is mere child's play and even folly compared with the true Christian's knowledge of Christ. For what is there that is truly wise or wonderful on earth compared with that amazing Mystery God manifest in the flesh? What will the men of Nazareth think when they shall see Him who made doors and windows for them, and to whom they paid day's wages, sitting on the great white throne?" And again: "If God takes me to-morrow out of this life, I will leave it as my dying testimony that I confess Jesus Christ to be both my Lord and my

God. And this I have learned, not from the Holy Scriptures only, but amid many sore temptations and hard experiences." "Venerable Father," said Justus Jonas to Luther, "do you die trusting in Christ as your God and your righteousness, and in the whole reformed doctrine you have constantly preached to us?" "Yes!" shouted Luther with his last breath. "Yes; Jesus Christ, my Lord and my Righteousness." Sings to us an English Catholic, and a true Lutheran in this :—

> Jesus is God! The solid earth,
>   The ocean broad and bright,
> The countless stars, like golden dust,
>   That strow the skies at night,
> The wheeling storm, the dreadful fire,
>   The pleasant, wholesome air,
> The summer's sun, the winter's frost,
>   His own creations were.
>
> Jesus is God! There never was
>   A time when He was not
> Boundless, Eternal, Merciful,
>   The Son the Sire begot!
> Backwards our thoughts through ages stretch,
>   Onwards through endless bliss,—
> For there are two eternities,
>   And both alike are His.
>
> Jesus is God! Let sorrow come,
>   And pain, and every ill;
> All are worth while, for all are means
>   His glory to fulfil.
> Worth while a thousand years of life
>   To speak one little word,
> If by our credo we might own
>   The GODHEAD of our LORD.

"A faith short of that," says Goodwin, "is but a Jewish, not to say a Turkish faith."

Now, since all that is so Scripturally true, just how, and just where, are we to begin to practise the Presence of CHRIST? Well, first, in the Four Gospels. For, just as God is in Christ, so is Christ in the Four Gospels. God has been made man in Jesus Christ; and, then, the Man Jesus Christ has been made visible, and audible, and tangible to us in Matthew, and Mark, and Luke, and John. They are John's own words on this great subject. "That which was from the beginning, which we have seen with our eyes, which we have heard, and our hands have handled of the Word of Life: even that Eternal Life which was with the Father, and which was manifested to us." Do you desire at any time to enter into the Presence of Christ? Well, then, just open the Four Gospels which the Holy Ghost has put into your hands for the purpose. Just open any of the Four Gospels, and take a believing heart with you into them, and see what will immediately take place in you. Open St. Matthew at the Sermon on the Mount and sit down at the Divine Preacher's feet and see and hear what you will immediately see, and hear, and feel, and confess. Again, open St. John at Jacob's well and immediately you will be back in the Presence of Christ, and will immediately, yourself, become the woman of Samaria with her guilty conscience and her thirsty heart. Yes, just open your New Testament anywhere, and immediately, according to your sinfulness, and according to your repentance, and according to your faith, so will it be that moment to you. One night when you so open your New Testament you will be Nicodemus alone in the secret Presence of Christ; another night you will be the Syrophœnician woman; another night Zacchæus; another night Martha and Mary; another night Peter; another night Mary Magdalene; another night Judas; another night the thief on the cross; another night Saul on his way to Damascus; and another night Paul's Epistles will all be so full of the Presence of Christ to you that your little sanctuary will be filled with His heavenly glory. Just keep the Gospels and the Epistles open before you, day and night, and see for yourselves.

And, then, take times of some length in which you go absolutely alone with the Gospels and the Epistles in your hand. For Christ seldom manifests His presence to us fully when we are in company; no, not even when we are in the best company. Leave all men, sometimes, even the best men, for the better practice of the Presence of Christ, just as He Himself did in the days of His flesh. For He was wont on occasion to leave all men, even Peter and James and John, and go out to solitary places in order that He might in those solitary places the better practise the Presence of His Father. And He did that till He was able to say that He was never alone for His Father was always with Him. And thus it was that at those seasons when all men went to their own homes, He, having no home of His own to which to go, went out and abode all night in the Presence of His Father in Gethsemane till the sun rose and He returned to His work in the Temple. Seek His Presence, then, sometimes in absolute, and not short, solitude.

But at all times and in all places be sure to seek His Presence in your own heart. Not at any time, nor in any place, but, always, in your own heart. Not even in the Four Gospels; not even in the Lord's Supper. For Christ's Presence is not in any of these things, nor in them all taken together, till His Presence is first in your own heart. In the long run, then, and in the most absolute reality, your own heart is Christ's true Presence Chamber; and He never will, no, nor ever can, manifest Himself anywhere else to you. Not in temples made with hands, but in that only true, and spiritual, and eternal temple, your own renewed, and clean, and holy, and heavenly heart. " Judas saith to Him, not Iscariot, Lord, how is it that Thou wilt manifest Thy Presence unto us, and not unto the world? Jesus answered and said to him, If a man love Me, he will keep My commandments. And My Father will love him: and We will come to him and will make our abode with him. Now, if ye know these things, happy are ye if ye do them."

You see, then, my brethren, how and where this great promise comes in: "Lo, I am with you alway." "Lo!" He said to His disciples, "I go away now in order that I may henceforth be with you always and everywhere." From His birth in Bethlehem up till now the Son of God had emptied Himself of all the power and glory of His Divine Nature and had been manifest to His disciples in their own limited human nature. But now that His time of humiliation and self-emptiness has come to an end He is to enter again upon all the divine glory He had with His Father before the world was. And, along with all else that He had laid down for a time, He is now, as the God-Man, Jesus Christ, to resume His Divine Attribute of omnipresence. Never, all His earthly days, could He have said, "Lo! I am with you alway." He could not have said that, for it was not, and it could not be, the case. When He was in Galilee, He could not be with His disciples in Jewry. And when He would go back to Galilee He must needs go through Samaria. And when He was beyond Jordan He could not be at Bethany with Martha and Mary and their sick brother Lazarus. And hence the expediency of His death, and resurrection, and ascension. So that, absent from them in His human body, He might be always with them in His Divine Spirit. Always with all His apostles; with Philip in Phrygia, and with Thomas in Parthia, and with Andrew in Scythia, and with Bartholomew in India, and with Gregory in Armenia, and with Boniface in Germany, and with Augustine in England, and with Patrick in Ireland, and with Columba in Scotland. "Christ's exaltation," says my college colleague, Professor Mackintosh, in his fine new book on "The Person of Christ": "Christ's exaltation has set Him free from all limitations, whether of place or of time. So that He is now accessible and available everywhere and always." "Deus ubique est, et totus ubique est," said

Augustine also. That is to say: God—and, in this case, Christ—is everywhere, and He is wholly everywhere: with us in this house at this hour; and, at this same hour, with our sons and daughters at the ends of the earth. With you at your bedside prayers this Sabbath night, and with me at mine.

> My footsteps, and my lying down,
>   Thou compassest always;
> Thou also most entirely art
>   Acquaint with all my ways.

Now, my brethren in Christ, be sure that from all this you take home with you these three lessons also. And first, never once see nor hear the Name of Christ without on the spot making a believing practice of His Presence. Learn to fill His hitherto too often idle and empty Name with all the fulness of His Divine Person and His Divine Presence. In the New Testament, in a Christian book, in a Christian hymn, in a sermon, in a prayer, in a grace at table, in the chance column of a periodical or a newspaper—never once see printed or hear spoken anywhere Christ's great Name without that moment seeing and hearing Himself. Practise unceasingly His Presence with you till you come to a great, a real, a personal, and a secret intimacy with Him, and till you are always with Him, and He always with you.

And then as many of you as always feel that you must have a sure hiding-place from the wrath and the contempt both of God and man and of your own conscience, practise without ceasing the Presence of the God-Man, Jesus Christ, the Rock of Ages, cleft for you. There are men among us who would much rather make away with themselves than they would be compelled to make a clean breast both of their conscience and of their heart before their fellow-men. But Jesus Christ is such a fellow-man that, instead of driving such men demented at the thought of standing naked and open before Him, He actually draws them all the more into His Presence, as into their one sure and safe city of refuge. And all such men learn to practise His saving and sheltering Presence as often as the shame, and the pain, and the remorse, and the terror, and the horror of their sins again find them out. And that is every day and every night they live.

> Rock of Ages, cleft for me,
> Let me hide myself in Thee.

Counselling a lady correspondent, the author of "The Practice of the Presence of God" wrote this: "Let us both learn to lift up our hearts to Him more than we have ever yet done. Even at our meals, let us not wholly forget Him. Nor when we are in company. For our least remembrance and recognition of Him is always acceptable to Him. And we need not be very loud, for He is always much nearer us than we think or will believe. And, thus, to be in His Presence there is no need to be continually in church. For, of our own hearts we may always make our best oratory, wherein to retire so as to hold the most intimate and loving intimacy with Him. Let us begin to-night then, for we have no time to lose. You are near sixty-four, I understand. And I am near eighty. Come away then, before it is too late. Now is the accepted time. Now is the day of salvation." Who of us will not say Amen to the old Carmelite's counsels? And who of us will not claim the fulfilment to ourselves of our Saviour's great promise, " Lo ! I am with you alway " ?

XXIII

BLOTTING OUT THE HANDWRITING THAT WAS AGAINST US

"HAVING forgiven you all trespasses,"—that, under the Gospel, is the simple fact; the simple, plain, and unadorned fact, simply, and plainly, and unadornedly stated. But it is the constant way of Holy Scripture to call in the aid of similitudes and metaphors and parables in order to give all the vividness and all the emphasis and all the impressiveness and all the homecomingness possible to the simple and plain facts of the Gospel. And the text is a most excellent case in point. For in the text the Apostle calls in the aid of this most impressive metaphor of a handwriting and says to us: You are forgiven all your trespasses, your Saviour having blotted out all the handwriting that was against you, which was contrary to you, and took it out of the way, nailing it to His Cross. Now, could truth and metaphor together further go? Could any conceivable truth and metaphor come more home to our sinful and fearful hearts?

Well, then, this metaphor of a handwriting, and a handwriting blotted out, though it remains a metaphor, is at the same time the greatest of all realities and the most blessed of all realities. As Thomas Goodwin says: "Though a book full of all manner of handwritings against us is a metaphor, yet you must know this for a certain and a sure rule in the interpretation of Scripture that all metaphors taken from outward and material things, and assumed up into spiritual and heavenly things: in that case the spiritual and the heavenly things are the true realities, while the outward and material things are but the unsubstantial shadows." That being so, a metaphor in Holy Scripture is very much what the Lord's Supper is among our means of grace to-day. You can get nothing in the Supper to-day that you have not already got in the Sermon. No. But in the Supper you get the Sermon over again, and that in a far more arresting and impressive way. As Robert Bruce said in one of his famous sermons on the Lord's Supper delivered in the High Kirk of Edinburgh in the year 1590, "Speers thou wherefore is the Sacrament annexed to the word seeing that we get nae mair in the Sacrament nor than we get in the word? Why, what mair can thy heart wish for, or imagine, than that great gift which God has already given thee in the Gospel? But the Sacrament is appointed us that we may get a better grip of that which we have already got. The Sacrament is appointed me, and is partaken of by me, in order that I may have Christ more fully received into my soul. This, there is nae doot, is the whole cause wherefore the seal is annexed to the evident of the simple word." And the very same thing exactly may be said concerning the metaphor in the text. You can never, never, get more than the full and free and immediate and everlasting forgiveness of all your trespasses. No. But when the Apostle having said that to you goes on to say this: "Jesus Christ having blotted out all the handwriting that was against you, which was contrary to you, and took it out of the way, nailing it to His Cross," then, as Robert Bruce says, by that way of re-stating and illustrating the Gospel fact you get a better grip of your forgiveness. That is to say, when you picture to yourself that so awful handwriting that was at one time so piled up against you, but which is now, and is for ever, blotted out in the blood of Christ, you thus get a much better sight and grip of your great forgiveness.

Now it is, no doubt, a very bold metaphor to say that Almighty God sets down in a written-out book a record of all our trepasses against Him and against our neighbour: and that, too, in His own Handwriting. But Holy Scripture says so, and is not afraid to say so. And the justification of such a bold anthropomorphism is seen in the fact that every Sabbath-school child knows quite well what that bold anthropomorphism means, and both the teacher and the child in their own conscience and in their own imagination justify the fearful words. Then, again, pursuing the same anthropomorphic metaphor, Holy Scripture solemnly warns us that we shall all be judged at the last day out of the things that are found written against us in the then opened book. And the Divine Pen that is every day making its entries against us all in those awful books is thus described to us for our warning: The word of God is quick and powerful, and sharper than any two-edged sword, piercing even to the dividing asunder of soul and spirit, and of the joints and marrow, and is a discerner of the thoughts and intents of the heart. Neither is there any creature that is not manifest in His sight; but all things are naked and opened to the eyes of Him with whom we have to do. It was all that awful penmanship copied out into John Flavel's conscience and heart which made that eminent saint to exclaim :—

> O conscience! who can stand against thy power!
> Endure thy gripes and agonies one hour!
> Stone, gout, strappado, racks, whatever is
> Dreadful to sense, are only toys to this!
> No pleasure, riches, honours, friends can tell
> How to give ease to this, 'tis like to hell.

But, granting for the moment that Almighty God's handwriting is a Scripture metaphor, there are many other handwritings against us, and contrary to us, that are no metaphor, but which are the actual and fearful fact. Let every grown-up man and woman look back and lay to heart how many actual handwritings of injured and angry men and women have been drawn out against them, first and last, and down to this day. How many injured and offended and angry men and women have written down your name and mine in their complaints and accusations against us. My brethren, when we are once truly broken and humbled in heart towards God and man, instead of resenting and retaliating upon any angry and accusing handwriting against us, we will at all heart-searching seasons like this often wonder that all men's accusations against us, both true and false, have not been proclaimed from the house-tops. And it is to such men among us that the Apostle has been commissioned to write this great Gospel passage. And it is from such men among us that he will get the response that his evangelical message so well deserves at our hands.

But all the time there are men among us whose cases were at one time far more fatal against them than all that. An accused man who boldly and truly denies everything else cannot deny his own handwriting when it is discovered and is produced against him. And the Bible is full of such self-incriminating handwritings, as if to warn all its self-inculpating readers. David's letter to Joab, written by his own royal hand, and stored up against him by his secret enemy who now had the king in his hands; Sennacherib's insulting letter to Hezekiah; Rehum the chancellor's letter to Artaxerxes; Jezebel's letter to the elders of Israel; Haman's letter to the governors of the provinces; Shemaiah's letter against the prophet; Saul's letters to Damascus; and, then, all the self-incriminating letters that we have written ourselves had they been all preserved and produced against us. And can you not put yourselves back to that communion morning in Colosse when this chapter was first read fresh from Paul's pen? For the hand writing-metaphor would come home to many consciences and hearts that morning, just as it does to many of our hearts at this Table this morning. What an uprush of praise to God would arise in their hearts, as, with the communion wine on their lips, they received the full assurance that all that had ever been written against them by other men, as well as all they had ever written against themselves, had all been for ever blotted out in the all-blotting-out blood of Christ. And this same glorious passage would be read every returning Sabbath morning in that little apostolic sanctuary, and would be repeated every day from house to house, till many men in Colosse who had hitherto turned a deaf ear to the Gospel preached in every other way were won at last by Paul's so powerful and so impressive and so peace-speaking metaphor of the blotted-out handwriting. As it is, no doubt, with many among ourselves to-day.

"And took it out of the way, nailing it to His Cross." Out of the way, that is, of God's coming to us with His great message of gracious reconciliation and of Gospel grace. And out of the way of our coming to God to be reconciled to Him and to be established in Gospel peace before Him for ever. Out of the way also of injured and angry men being reconciled to us, and our being reconciled to them. That awful handwriting, so long as it lasted, stood absolutely blocking up our way to peace with God and with man and with ourselves. It stood also absolutely blocking our way to the possession and the enjoyment of all that we now possess and enjoy in this life; and much more absolutely blocking up our way to all that we shall possess and enjoy in the life to come. But now Jesus Christ, our Surety, our Substitute, our sin-atoning Sacrifice, our Daysman, and our Great High Priest, has taken every syllable of that evil handwriting against us and has nailed it all to His Cross. If you had stood on the street of Jerusalem that great Passover Day you would have seen three condemned men led out to Calvary to their crucifixion and each one of the three with all his accusations written in a large handwriting and hanging exposed upon his breast. The two thieves had all their thefts and all their other crimes written in a large handwriting and exposed upon their breasts for all men to read; after which that awful handwriting was nailed to their crosses that all men might see the righteousness of their crucifixion. And the third Malefactor had all His accusations also written out and hung upon His breast, and nailed to His Cross in the same way. Only, His accusations were written in Hebrew and Greek and Latin: Pilate being a prophet in that handwriting of his: God guiding his hand. Pilate knew not what he wrote. But God knew. He read all the languages, past and present, and all the world over, in which any accusations had been, or ever would ever be, written against any of His people; and, in ways past our finding out, in ways known only to His own wisdom and grace,

God made all those handwritings, both true and false, to meet on our Redeemer's breast, and cross, and head, and heart, that great Atonement Day. So much so that when our Surety and Substitute and Sacrifice received the vinegar, He said, It is finished. For by that time He had made an end of all the handwritings that ever were or ever would be laid against any and all of His redeemed. And then, on the third day after, He brought in an everlasting righteousness. And that so as to make and to show God just as often as He justified the ungodly. What I have written I have written, said the prophet, not knowing what he wrote.

But, with all that, I find nothing that rises to heaven so often in Bishop Andrewes' private prayers as this terrified cry: "Reserve not any evil handwriting against me!" Night after night, week after week, and year after year, the handwritings of God and man against that great saint came back and rose up continually in such large and angry letters before his sleepless conscience that this agonizing prayer was never for long out of his mouth: "O God, reserve not any evil handwriting against Thy broken-hearted servant. For mine iniquities are increased over mine head, and my trespass is grown up into the heavens. Since the days of my youth I have been in a great trespass, even unto this day. O my God, reserve no evil handwriting to leap to the light to condemn me!" But then, like all such true and lifelong penitents, I find Andrewes winding up every new week of penitential prayer and holy living with this Gospel Doxology, which I give you to take home with you in his own handwriting :—

"O Lord, my Lord, for my being, life, reason; for nurture, protection, guidance; for education, civil rights, religion; for Thy gifts of grace, nature, fortune; for redemption, regeneration, instruction; for my call, recall, yea, many calls besides; for Thy forbearance, long-suffering, long long-suffering toward me, many seasons, many years; for all good things received, successes granted me, good things done; for my parents, honest and good; teachers, kind; benefactors, never to be forgotten; fellow-ministers of one mind; hearers thoughtful; friends sincere; domestics faithful; for all who have advantaged me by books, sermons, conversations, prayers, examples, rebukes, even injuries; for all these, and all others which I know, and which I know not; open, hidden, remembered, forgotten, done when I wished, and when I wished not,—for all that I praise Thee, and will praise; I bless Thee, and will bless; I give thanks to Thee, and will give thanks all the days of my life. For who am I, or what is my father's house, that Thou shouldest look upon such a dead dog as I am? What shall I render to the Lord for all His benefits toward me? For all things in which He has spared me until now? Holy, Holy, Holy! Thou art worthy, O Lord our God, to receive glory and honour and power, for Thou hast created all things, and for Thy pleasure they are and were created. Behold, the Tabernacle of God is with men, and He will dwell with them, and they shall be His people, and God Himself shall

BLOTTING OUT THE HANDWRITING 211

be with them, and shall wipe away all tears from their eyes. And there shall be no more death, neither sorrow, nor crying. Neither shall there be any more pain, for the former things are all passed away. And He said to me, Write, for these things are true and faithful."

XXIV

HUMILITY THROUGH MANY HUMILIATIONS

TO begin with, and that we may clearly understand what it is we are speaking about, just what is humility? Etymologically, and morally, and experimentally, and evangelically studied, just what is that Christian grace which is called humility, which is so essential to the Christian character, which is so praised in the Holy Scriptures, and which is to be so recognised and rewarded by God? Well, when it is studied etymologically humility is discovered to be derived from *humus*, the ground. A derivation that has its own deep and manifold significance to the thoughtful student.

And now to examine into true Christian humility, and to examine into it at its true Source, which is the Son of God, Jesus Christ. And I do not know that we can do better than to begin with the twenty-eighth question and answer in the Westminster Shorter Catechism, which runs thus: " Wherein did Christ's humiliation consist? Christ's humiliation consisted in His being born, and that in a low condition, made under the law, undergoing the miseries of this life, the wrath of God, and the cursed death of the Cross." "In His being born, and that in a low condition." Do you ever take it home to yourselves, and think about it?—that the Eternal Son of God, the true and only Maker of Heaven and earth, humbled Himself to be born in a stable and to be laid in a manger! "Foxes have holes," He said in His life-long poverty, "and the birds of the air have nests, but the Son of Man hath not where to lay His head." And, then, He underwent "all the miseries of this life." On that Goodwin has this: "Christ was indeed *Vir dolorum*—the Man of sorrows, which sorrows did so wear Him out and waste Him that He looked nearer fifty years old than the thirty years He was. And no wonder. For never was any man so put to it as He was. Divine wisdom to have to converse all those years with human folly; absolute and spotless holiness with universal sinfulness; and absolute and essential truth with all manner of error and ignorance and slowness of heart. Contrarieties and antipathies of disposition in our relatives," says that great preacher, "how burdensome to us are all these things, and how glad we would be to get rid of them all! But if He had chosen to stick to it He might have had much more suitable society in Heaven than He ever had down here on earth. He might have had Abraham and Isaac and Jacob to converse with; and Moses and David and Isaiah, and with angels to wait upon Him and His saints. But no; He humbled Himself to all that we read in the Four Gospels." And then, "the wrath of God." Not against Himself, indeed; that was impossible. But all the more against all our wrath-deserving sins that were laid upon Him. "The wrath of God," says Jacob Behmen, "a word intolerable, but unavoidable."

Now from His birth at Bethlehem down to His death at Jerusalem, through all the thirty-three years of His earthly life, our Lord was learning ever more and more humility through all the humiliations that were continually heaped upon Him. Our Lord's humility was not perfect till He had humbly and obediently endured and performed all His divinely ordained humiliations down to the very lowest and last of them. His humility of mind when He was twelve years old was quite perfect enough for His twelve years. But He was not so exercised and so perfected in His humility at twelve years old as He was when He began to be about thirty years old. The daily and hourly humiliations He suffered in His mother's house and in Joseph's workshop and elsewhere during all those years, only prepared Him for the far greater humiliations of His public life, and for His so humiliating death. And just as He was, so are we who are His disciples. We, like Him, only attain to our true humility through a lifetime of divinely ordained humiliations. Our Lord's first humiliation on earth was His being born, and that in a low condition. Now, all His followers do not have that forerunning humiliation of His ordained to them. It is only some specially chosen men who have that eminent opportunity ordained and offered to them.

And, then, there were some absolutely nameless humiliations connected with our Lord's birth of His mother—absolutely nameless humiliations that are but dimly and remotely hinted at in the reverential Gospels. And those aggravated humiliations of His are but dimly hinted at and are then left in order that those followers of His who can read between the lines may find out those nameless humiliations of His to their greater adoration of their Redeemer-Forerunner and to their own greater attainments in His amazing humility.

Then, again, what an ever-welling spring of humility we all have in the ever-present remembrance of our foolish and ill-advised speeches that are scattered all up and down our past life. We blush scarlet as often as we remember the people who will never forget the things they heard us say; so utterly foolish were those things; so stupid, and so far worse than stupid. What a rich web of things some of us have simply in our past speeches—enough if we will only recall them and lay them to heart to clothe us all the rest of our days, and from head to foot, with shame and with humility. And, still more, whole multitudes of humiliating words and things that never came out to the eyes or the ears of our fellow-men. Says the "Serious Call" to us on this subject: "All virtue is founded in truth; and so our humility is founded in a true and just sense of our weakness, misery, and sin. He who rightly sees and feels his sinful condition will always live in humility. Let any man but take this view of his own life, and he will see reason enough to confess that pride was not made for such men as he is. Let him but consider that if the world but knew all that of him which he knows of himself; if they saw what vanity governs his inside, and what secret tempers sully and corrupt his best actions, he would lose all pretence to be honoured and admired for his goodness and his wisdom. This is so true, that nothing would appear more dreadful to such men than to have their hearts fully disclosed to the eyes of all beholders. And, perhaps, there are few people in the world who would not rather die than have all their secret follies, the vanities of their minds, the falseness of their pretences, their uneasiness, hatred, envy, and vexation made known to all the world. And shall pride be entertained in a heart thus conscious of its own miserable behaviour?" Pascal, again, is nowhere so pungent as when he is handling the "disproportion of man." Man's disproportion, Pascal means, to his original greatness. His lack of truth, and of wisdom, and of integrity, and of true holiness. His pretences and his postures compared with his real worth and value. But it is only when we learn to read ourselves into Pascal's disproportion that we arrive at anything of that deep humility with which that great man was always clothed himself, and with which he has clothed so many of his overmastered and captivated readers. The deep disproportion between their office in life and their real selves; between what they fain would have all men think of them and what they in reality are; between what they think of themselves, and what God thinks of them, and will one day discover them to be. There are no such humiliating, but at the same time such healing pages in all religious literature as in Pascal's thoughts on the disproportion of man, and in William Law's heart-searching writings. Candidates for a heavenly humility! As Coleridge said, Sell your soft bed and buy Blaise Pascal and William Law.

No, this can never be enough dwelt upon by Paul, or by Pascal, or by Law, or by anyone else; this, that nothing so humbles a man as his own inward, or, as Paul calls it, his indwelling sinfulness. And thus, it may almost be said, how happy are we that this is so. Since we all have so much indwelling sinfulness, and in that so much possibility and potentiality of evangelical humility. When Paul was in danger of being too much puffed up because he had been promoted to such unparalleled visions and revelations of the Lord, how was he secured from spiritual pride? "Lest I should be exalted above measure through the abundance of the revelations, there was given me a thorn in the flesh, the messenger of Satan to buffet me, lest I should be exalted above measure." Now, some commentators have thought that Paul's heart-humbling thorn was epilepsy, some ophthalmia, some an oft-recurring attack of an Asiatic sickness. For my part I have never been able to see how any one of these things—no, nor all of them taken together—could ever have humbled Paul's proud heart as it was always humbled. I wholly agree with Paul's great Puritan expositor who finds Paul's best security against a high mind described in the seventh of the Romans. Yes, that great chapter was always Paul's own private looking-glass in which he always saw what manner of man he really was—visions of paradise and all. Yes, if St Paul's lifelong instrument of humiliation was a thorn at all, then it was a thorn taken from Christ's crown of thorns, and set deep into the Apostle's sinful heart. Christ's ever-increasing humility came at last to its completion and crown on the Cross. And so did Paul's corresponding humility in his corresponding cross also.

But if you would know it, my brethren, a lifetime of unceasing and ever-deepening prayer is by far the best security against pride, and by far the best guarantee of a genuine evangelical humility. I feel sure of this, that every truly spiritually-minded man among you experiences his greatest humiliation when he is alone with God in secret prayer. The things he has still to pray for; the things he has still to confess; the things the mere mention of which lays him down in the dust of death; yes, his secret time and place of prayer is the spiritual man's most heart-searching valley of humiliation. O you, therefore, who have been chosen and called to prosecute a life of spiritual humility frequent, continually, your secret place and time of prayer. And have no secrets with God or with yourself then and there. Pray on in secret, says Christ to you; pray on and on and never faint, whatever your confession of sin may have to be, and whatever your petition for a new and a clean heart. A deeper

HUMILITY THROUGH HUMILIATIONS

and an ever deeper humility was always the burden of William Law's secret prayer at the third hour of every day. Law's work lay largely in philosophical and theological controversy, and he felt a mighty want of humility in his continual intercourse with controversial men and with their controversial writings. And, full of pride and scorn and contempt and ill-will as he knew himself to be, he felt a wondrous change coming over his spirit as he prayed year after year and every day of the year, secretly, expressly, particularly, and pleading instances, for the heavenly-minded grace of humility.

True humility, then, is the very foundation-stone of the whole edifice of the Christian character. " I was always exceedingly pleased with that saying of Chrysostom," says Calvin, " ' The foundation of all our philosophy is humility!' And yet more pleased with that of Augustine, ' As,' says he, ' the great orator being asked what was the first thing in the rules of eloquence, he answered delivery. What is the second thing, he answered delivery. What is the third thing, still he answered delivery. So, says Augustine, if you ask me concerning the graces of the Christian character, I will answer—firstly, secondly, thirdly, and for ever humility.' " Yes, surely. And thus it is that God so orders all our lives as to teach and train us in true humility every day we live. Every day He causes men to ride over our heads. Every day He makes men to be promoted and preferred before us. Every day we make mistakes and commit blunders and do wrongs, and He has men of His ready and lying in wait to correct us rudely and to advertise our errors and mistakes and trespasses to the whole world. And so on, and so on, till our whole life is one High School and Academy of humiliation and of consequent humility, if we will only enter that great school, and will pay the impoverishing fees of it, and will every day learn the appointed lessons of it, and will never play truant away from it. And, thus, the more we learn our daily lessons in true humility, the more will we be able to learn more and more all our appointed humiliations to the greater and ever greater perfection of our Christlike character.

For Greatheart's experience in the Valley of Humiliation, and Christian's, and Mercy's, and Mr Fearing's and the Shepherd Boy's song, consult John Bunyan's masterpiece of spiritual truth and literary beauty, the " Pilgrim's Progress," Parts first and second.

XXV

YE HAVE NEED OF PATIENCE

TO begin with, and to begin at the beginning, God Himself has need of patience. And God has said as much concerning Himself on many recorded occasions and it is written of Him in a multitude of Old Testament Scriptures. So much so that the Old Testament might very well be described as the Book of God's patience with all men, and especially with His own people Israel. The hundred and third Psalm celebrates God's great patience with His own people in one of the most beautiful Scriptures that ever were written. That wonderful Scripture of God's patience runs thus: " The Lord is slow to anger, and plenteous in mercy. He will not always chide, neither will He keep His anger for ever. He hath not dealt with us after our sins, nor hath He rewarded us according to our inquities." And every time we sing that experimental Psalm of the Divine patience we see ourselves in it as in a heavenly glass, till we hear the Apostle saying to us: " Now the God of all patience grant you to be likeminded toward one another, according to Christ Jesus." Yes;

God Himself has the greatest need of patience, and He has never failed in the exercise of an infinite patience toward His own people; no, nor never will fail.

Then, again, no reader of the New Testament can ever forget how great need of patience our Lord had even with His most chosen disciples. Indeed, they so drew upon His stock of patience that they seemed, sometimes, almost to exhaust it altogether. What a strain must have been put upon our Lord's patience with the twelve before He felt compelled to give utterance to these terrible words to them: "Oh, faithless and perverse generation! How long shall I be with you? How long shall I suffer you?" But, then, a lifetime of such patience on earth only made His great patience more and more perfect; till now, in heaven, He is able to wait patiently for His Father's time for the complete fulfilment of all His Father's promises to Him; such promises as this: "Ask of Me, and I shall give thee the heathen for thine inheritance, and the uttermost parts of the earth for thy possession." And this: "He shall have dominion also from sea to sea; and from the river to the ends of the earth." And this: "His name shall endure for ever; His name shall be continued as long as the sun; and men shall be blessed in Him, till all men shall call Him blessed." As He remembers all these still unfulfilled promises, I seem to hear Him saying, but saying it with a Son's perfected patience: Thy will be done; but make no tarrying, O My Father.

Now, following up all that, there is nothing of

which we ourselves have so much need as just this same great gift and grace of patience. And, to begin with, as God has great need of patience with us, even so we have great need of patience with Him. That may sound a far too bold thing for me to say; but just recall what is said and sung so often in the Holy Scriptures concerning the patience of God's ancient people with their covenant God. In the twenty-fifth Psalm we have this so patient prayer offered up: "Lead me in Thy truth, and teach me; for on Thee do I wait all the day." And in the thirty-seventh Psalm we have this: "Rest in the Lord, and wait patiently for Him. Fret not thyself; but commit thy way unto the Lord, and keep on trusting in Him." And in the fortieth Psalm we have this amazing exercise of David's patience with God: "I waited patiently, when I was all the time sunk in an horrible pit, and in the miry clay. And, for my patience, as I lay in those awful depths, He inclined to me and heard my cry."

> My soul, wait thou with patience
> Upon thy God alone;
> On Him dependeth all my hope
> And expectation.

And thus we ourselves must learn to have a lifelong patience with God, and especially like David in the matter of still unanswered prayer. When we are tempted to complain that our most importunate prayer still lies before God wholly unanswered: for one thing we are to be patient and are to bethink ourselves how much the Hearer of prayer has upon His hands; how much besides us and our affairs. We and our affairs are not God's only charge and care. We and our affairs are mixed up in a thousand ways with other praying people and with their pressing and importunate affairs; and we must learn to take our turn, and to wait with patience till God sees good to give us our answer; and that in a way that will not hurt those other praying people of His. Let us wait on the Lord and give Him time, and He will not tarry one hour after our case and our neighbour's case are both ready for the right solution. An old Hebrew prophet was exactly in our case when God taught him to say, "I will stand upon my watch, and will set me upon my tower, and will wait to see what He will say to me. And the Lord answered me, and said: 'The vision is yet for an appointed time, but at the end it shall speak, and shall not lie: though it tarry, wait for it: because it will surely come; it will not tarry. But the just shall live by his faith and his patience.'"

And then we must have patience with ourselves. For an instance of that: I must not lose patience with myself, I must not become downhearted and desert my pulpit because I cannot preach like Newman or Spurgeon. I must not fret myself because my parish is not the whole world, like John Wesley's parish. My brethren, you may not know it, but this proud impatience with themselves, and with their small talents, and with their small spheres, has in past times been the ruin of many of our ministers, and it is ruining many of them at the present moment. Nor must I be too impatient because of the slowness of my personal sanctification. I must not despair of my final and full sanctification because I have not yet attained to it, neither am already perfect in it. I must learn to be patient both with my imperfect intellectual equipment and with my poor spiritual attainment. Says Thomas Goodwin on this subject : " To climb up the difficult hill of our daily duties without weariness, to keep on and on in a straight path, and not to pick and choose our way, and not to faint or sink in our hearts—that needs an amount of patience that few of us as yet possess." And the always fresh and clear-eyed and sagacious Bishop Martensen has a whole chapter, but I must content myself with giving you the mere title of it. The title is : " Compassion with ourselves ; patience and endurance, and long-suffering with ourselves."

And then we have need of patience, actually, with all men. Indeed, " all men " is the Apostle's very word in this matter. " Now, we beseech you, brethren," he writes, " be patient with all men." But, first and always, let us learn to be patient with the members of our own household. For the family is the great high-school and exercising-ground of patience. In the very best family life there is constant need of an even temper and a patient and a tranquil mind. Presence of mind is a great virtue everywhere, and in everything ; but nowhere more than just in the everyday intercourse and conversation of family life. Presence of mind to say at the right moment just what we ought to say. Presence of mind to count ten before we speak at all, and a hundred before we speak what we can never recall.

> Prune thou thy words, the thoughts control
> That o'er thee swell and throng;
> They will condense within thy soul,
> And change to purpose strong.

Now, new beginners in family life, and those not yet properly begun, will be sure to say to me: "What! do you mean to preach to us such a cold and commonplace thing as patience, when our hearts are running over with the warm and generous and exuberant love of the bridegroom and the bride?" Yes, sir, I do; I solemnly do. For common sense and universal experience combine to warn you that no amount of youthful and exuberant love is enough, till it bears its seasonable fruit in patience and in consideration of one another; aye, and even in an ever-ready self-sacrifice. Patience with one another is the very last virtue that young people look forward to need when they are still dreaming about the absolutely unclouded happiness that they are to have in their married life. But however many good qualities of mind and of heart and of character any young husband or wife may have, no human being is so perfect in this world as not to have need of patience. The wisest of us and the best of us have many defects in our manners, and in our habits, and in our ways of thinking and speaking and acting; many defects that tempt, and try, and sometimes even torture, those who live nearest us, and who love us most. Settle then, and settle early with yourselves that with all your love and honour to one another you are still on earth, and are not yet in heaven; and that as you have not brought absolute perfection to your side of the house you are not so foolish as to demand absolute perfection on the other side. With all your good intentions and high resolutions you have still your own share of what has caused disappointment and distress, and sometimes distaste and dislike and utter alienation of heart, in so many once happy homes. And, with God's help, determine that should patience and forbearance, in great things or in small, be ever needed in your house, it shall not be wanting on your part. " Husbands, love your wives: even as Christ loved the Church, and gave Himself for it." And, " Children, obey your parents in the Lord, for this is right. Honour thy father and thy mother, that it may be well with thee, and that thou mayest live long on the earth. And, ye fathers, provoke not your children to anger; but bring them up in the nurture and admonition of the Lord." There is a whole world of wisdom in that one word, " Provoke not your children to anger "; and that one word has a thousand applications to all who are the fathers of children. And then, all who are the fathers and mothers of children have need to keep in mind that law of nature, that law of grace, that law of God—that it is first the blade, and then the ear, and then the full corn in the ear. And that they are not to look for the full ear in childhood, no nor even in early youth. But they are to be like the husbandman who waiteth for the precious fruit of the earth, and hath long patience for it, until he receive the early and latter rain.

And then, as family life goes on, the time comes in some families when the grown-up sons and daughters need no little patience with their parents. At this point I cannot take home to my own house, and offer to yours, anything better than this out of Christina Rossetti: "Distaste," says that wise writer, "simple distaste will soon vitiate our due observance of the Fifth Commandment. Our parents speak when we wish they would be silent. Their manners also are old-fashioned, and their taste so lacks refinement. Their opinions are behind the age, and their standards of measurement are prejudiced and narrow. They know nothing of the present day; they do not even wish to know any person or anything worth knowing. And then we, their sons and daughters, habitually stand in an attitude of self-defence and opposition. We are critics and censors at home, and not true children. At our best, we but tolerate what we cannot reform." So far that fine spiritual and ethical writer. The sum is that parents and children, as long as they are still under the same roof, will have no little need of patience with one another. But then, when patience has her perfect work,—then how peaceful, how harmonious, and how happy is that Christian home!

There is a passage in the Colossians that has often made me stop and think and wonder. That passage runs thus: " Timotheus and I do not cease to pray for you that ye may be strengthened with all might, according to the glorious power of God, unto all patience and long-suffering, with joyfulness." That is to say, all our patience and long-suffering with one another is the result of God's glorious power working in us. That is to say, every single instance of our patience and long-suffering at home is not so much our patience and long-suffering as it is the glorious power of God put forth upon us. That is something for us all to take home with us from this House of God this morning. To remember that in every thought and word and deed of patience and long-suffering with one another we are all the time being strengthened with nothing less than the great strength of God. So that when we see someone's face in our family flush scarlet with sudden anger at some unkind or unjust or injurious word or deed, and then see that same hot flush pass off without any angry or retaliating word being spoken in return, in that we are told to see nothing less than the sudden, if unseen, working of God's glorious power. For, according to this Scripture, God's most glorious power is best seen in our constant and instant self-command and self-suppression, and in our patience and long-suffering with one another. And, more than that, if we rise to this and attain to this, to be patient and long-suffering, with joyfulness, then, in that case, we are walking worthy of the Lord to all well-pleasing, and are thus increasing in the true knowledge of God. And all that at home, mind you. Yes, at home; and not away out and far away from home in some high-sounding deed of miracle and martyrdom. Not in the ends of the earth, but in the patience and long-suffering of our everyday life, among our own household. I will repeat that wonderful passage, and will leave it with you to make experiment upon its truth and it blessedness in your own house this very day and every day. "We do not cease to pray for you that ye might walk worthy of the Lord, being strengthened with all might, according to His glorious power, unto all patience and long-suffering, with joyfulness. Giving thanks to the Father who hath made us meet to be partakers of the inheritance of the saints in light, and who hath delivered us from the power of darkness, and hath translated us into the Kingdom of His dear Son."

XXVI

I

THAT great Divine Name "I AM" contains far more divine truth than we are able to receive. But, while that is so, that great Divine Name may perhaps be paraphrased and interpreted to some extent in this way: that great Divine Name I Am is so announced and proclaimed to us in order to teach us that God alone truly and properly exists; that He alone essentially and necessarily and eternally exists. And accordingly that all other so-called existences of all kinds have their true source and their only origin in Him. That great Name I Am labours to express that which can never be adequately expressed; no, not even by the pen of a prophet specially raised up and specially experienced and specially inspired for the purpose. I Am in the Hebrew tongue was intended to embody and to proclaim the true and the alone Godhead of Israel's God. And thus it was that Jehovah, I Am, was the distinguishing mark and the divine seal of the whole Mosaic faith and worship and obedience. And thus this heaven-given Name was stamped, so to say, from the very beginning, upon the mind and upon the imagination and upon the conscience and upon the heart of the whole Hebrew people; and then through their prophets and their psalmists upon the mind and upon the imagination and upon the conscience and upon the heart of all mankind who have ever worshipped and trusted and obeyed the one only and true God. And then the somewhat more expanded and enlarged Name I Am that I Am is but a further effort to express God's eternity, His everlastingness, and His unchangeableness. "I Am that I Am," says St. Augustine, "is the God-given Name of the eternally unchangeable Divine Nature. I Am that I Am serves to indicate a kind of existence that no one has ever possessed, or ever will possess, but the one only and true God." "God's great Name Jehovah," says Thomas Goodwin, "stands on the page of Holy Scripture as inflexible, and as grammatically indeclinable, as His Divine Nature is immutable. God's great Name Jah holds its supreme and unique place far above all other names; and it sovereignly refuses to become subject to any of the laws or rules of either heavenly or earthly grammar." Truly, then, and properly and ultimately God alone can say I Am. And if any of His creatures, the greatest and the best, are able to say that they are, that is so because they live and move and have all their being in and under the great I Am Himself.

But with all that it will be remembered that the Man Christ Jesus once said of Himself, I and My Father are one: and again, Before Abraham was I Am. And by that by far the greatest of all His great sayings concerning Himself our Divine Lord intends us to understand that He and His Father are One in their Divine Nature : " The same in substance," as the great creeds and the great catechisms have it ; and, thus, are the same in all their Divine power and glory. For, even when the Divine and Eternal Son " emptied Himself " of all His Divine power and glory and lived among men a life of faith and prayer and holy obedience, even so, all the time He remained in Himself, in His Divine Personality and Individuality, what He had eternally been, and everlastingly will be, the Godhead Son of the Godhead Father : and thus one in everything with His Father. And that Oneness held and obtained even when He had laid down all His Godhead power and glory for a season in order that in His estate of self-depletion and humiliation He might redeem us back to God with His own blood ; and so make us partakers for ever of His own Sonship and heirship and everlasting life.

Now, to advance and to go forward from all that, both Scripturally and experimentally. Just as God Himself looks at all things and measures all things by the standard of His own Divine Personality; and just as Jesus Christ, both in His Godhead and in His Manhood, does the same thing : even so, we are made in their divine image in that respect also. For we also look at all things and measure all things by the one standard of our own personality and individuality and experience. It was a first principle of a great Greek philosopher that "Man is the measure of all things." And, though we may shrink back somewhat from the full boldness and the full sweep of that great Protagorean principle, at the same time that great principle humbly and devoutly employed will, in not a few ways, help us in our further study of ourselves and of the things that most concern ourselves.

And now in application of that great principle, let us take our stand, each several one of us, upon our own absolute personality, and individuality, and experience; and from that sure and clear and safe centre let us open our eyes and look out at the whole world of men and things that opens to each one of us all around us. And on this principle I will make bold to speak first of what I myself see and feel and have to say to you. For my own personality, and individuality, and experience is the only personality, and individuality, and experience that I really know, and can safely take my stand upon. And, then, *cor ad cor*, heart to heart, as Cardinal Newman chose for his coat-of-arms, and for the supreme principle and rule of all his remaining preaching.

Well, then, when I open my eyes and look all around me, what do I see? I see, on the one hand, so many innocent-looking, so many light-hearted, and so happy-looking lives that so many men and women are living. Whereas, on the other hand, I cannot but see the sorely burdened, cross-bearing, and cup-drinking lives that so many other men and women are living. And both classes of people, to all appearance, all but wholly without the sanctification and the support and the comfort of a personal faith and hope in the living God, and of a personal hold of His Son Jesus Christ as their Redeemer. It is only one here and another there who seem to know or feel their need of a Redeemer, or of anything of that kind. And as I look and look on all that and ponder and ponder all that, I am sometimes terribly shaken in my faith in the love, and in the wisdom, and in the power of God. The lives of so many men and women all around me are to my eyes so absolutely unlike, and so wholly out of keeping with, what Holy Scripture proclaims concerning all men, both in their joys and in their sorrows. There are so few people who seem to feel any need for or to have found any room for the religion and the life of redemption; so few that I am sometimes driven to doubt the real truth of the Bible representations of redemption, and of all men's absolute need of the Bible redemption. But, then, as soon as I turn away from this faith-entangling and faith-perplexing world all around me, and descend down into the inner world of my own mind and heart and conscience, that moment I find within myself a whole world of things that immediately makes me a firmer believer than ever in all the revealed things of God. I always find accumulated within myself the most conclusive proof and the most infallible assurance of the wisdom and the grace and the power of God in the Gospel. As also of the overwhelming need of man, of one man at any rate, for the salvation of God; the absolute and overwhelming need of one man, and he the only man that I know much about. Entering in that way into myself I am immediately to myself the true and the full measure both of the outward world around me, and of the inward world within me, and of the great world of God and His Son Jesus Christ above me. Let me repeat all that, and let me enlarge upon all that, since it is so absolutely and so incontestably true and so all-essential to me and to you. Well, then, when I see all around me the innocence and the sweetness of little children, and the uplifting and joyous hopes of their parents, and the generous-heartedness of young people just entering upon their so hopeful life; as also when I see the many splendid deeds of devotion and self-sacrifice of which the world, at its worst, is full, and many more suchlike things, I confess that the sight of all that sometimes tempts me in certain moods of mind and in certain companies, to feel somewhat ashamed of the Gospel of Christ and of Christ Himself. And that because both Christ and the Gospel always begin by taking such a severe and such a sad view of human life; such a severe and such a sad view of the universal sinfulness of all men; and thus assert the absolute necessity for the sin-atoning death of the Son of God; as also the absolute and universal need of a new birth, and a lifelong conflict with sin, even in the case of the very best men. The seemingly abounding joys of life on the one hand, and then the much more abounding sorrows of life on the other hand,—these things have made many men to become almost infidels as regards the existence and the wisdom and the power and the love of God. Even as all these things long enough brooded over might well have made me one of them had I not learned long ago to say things like this to myself continually: "Sir," I say to myself, "look well within before you make up your mind on these outward and remote matters. Attend first to yourself and to the far darker problems of your own soul. Concentrate your attention on the constant and secret workings of your own heart. The outward world of all mankind is far too large for you to grasp and to master and to philosophise upon and to dogmatise upon. Be thankful that both you and the whole world are in the hands of Him whose understanding is infinite and whose love is even more so." And, then, as often as I again hear and obey that divine voice and descend down into myself, then, were I alone in the world—as, indeed, I am—and were the whole world at war with my faith, as indeed it is: even so, I for one would feel myself continually shut up to the faith of Christ and to all that the faith of Christ contains and proclaims for me. Beset behind and before as I am with all manner of difficulties and doubts, with absolutely unfathomable mysteries concerning both God and man and myself, at the same time amid all that I remain myself. Amid all these things I am who and what I am. And, being who and what I am, I absolutely need and I absolutely demand and I absolutely cannot part with one single syllable of the truth as it is in Jesus. And thus as long as I am who and what I am, a thousand outward worlds, and every one of them as full as it could hold of trials to faith and temptations to unbelief,—all that would only make me retreat the more into the only refuge and sure hiding-place for me and for my faith : even Almighty God Himself, and His great salvation in His Son Jesus Christ. Yes, my own inward sinfulness and manifold misery settles, and settles for ever, this whole matter for me. "I acknowledge that I am fallible," says John Newton, "yet I must lay claim to a certainty about the way of salvation. I am as sure of some things in the way of salvation as I am of my own existence. And I should be so if there was no human being upon earth but myself. I am under no more doubt about the way of my salvation than I have of the way from Olney to London." I agree with every word of the old laird of Brodie also, as he tells himself how his own personal experiences of sin and of salvation had made him and had kept him a believing man. In a diary scarcely second to the "Confessions" itself, Lord Brodie writes thus concerning himself : "O my God, Thy love and grace to me ! I dare never question all Thy love and all Thy grace to me, past, present, and yet to come. Ere I come to my journey's end ; and even already what free grace from Thee to me !

What free grace in pardoning, what in preventing, what in convincing, what in enlightening, what in strengthening and confirming and upholding, what in watering and making me to grow, what in knowledge, faith, experience, patience, mortification, uprightness, stedfastness, watchfulness, humiliation, resolution, self-denial, discovery of snares and avoiding them, what for my public life, what for my private life, what for grace and strength against pitfalls on the right hand and on the left." Yes, I take my stand alongside of old Brodie; and if he had not written that book of blood and tears and prayers and praises, I would have taken pen in hand myself, and, indeed, may yet do so.

And it is the very same with me as often as, after opening myself, I go on to open my Bible. I am what I am; and, as Coleridge says, my Bible always finds me, and I always find myself in my Bible, till I am rejoiced above all measure to see and to say continually that He who made me must have had my Bible made for me. And my Bible alone of all my books. As I sit and write these lines I am surrounded and overwhelmed with a houseful of books of all kinds; but the longer I live, and the older I grow, they are less and less in my hands, and take up less and less of my remaining time. And that is so, because so few of them seem at all to know me, and to be able to speak home to me. My Shakespeare finds me in many things. But he has never found me in my deepest things. He has everything that is in me; everything but my unspeakable sinfulness and God's unspeakable salvation; and thus Shakespeare is the Bible of the natural man, while the Bible is the Shakespeare of the spiritual man. If Shakespeare had had my sinfulness and God's salvation I would then have had a second Apostle Paul in my own tongue wherein I was born. But that was not appointed to be. There is but one Paul, and there is but one Bible. And my Bible to me is complete and supreme and alone. Till, the longer I live, the more I concentrate upon my Bible, and upon my few books that draw their truth and their power from my Bible and from the Bible experiences and Bible attainments of its great authors. Every time I open it I find Jesus Christ in my Bible. And He answers to me in every word He speaks, and in every deed He does. And above all His words He answers to me in His ever-blessed words of pardon and peace to me. And above all His deeds His death on the sin-atoning Cross for me. Christ, and His sin-atoning blood; Christ, and His imputed righteousness, as the Apostle always has it; it is because my Bible is so full of Him, and of these two supreme things of His—it is this that makes it the Book of all my books to me.

Now, my brethren, for one thing out of a thousand such things, all this should enable us to sing our great hymn "Just as I am" with the spirit, and with the understanding, and with the imagination also. And if we once begin to sing that great evangelical hymn in that way, we will never cease singing it till we see the great

I AM HIMSELF, and are made for ever like Him. As thus :—

> Just as I am, though tossed about
> With many a conflict, many a doubt,
> Fightings and fears within, without,
>   O Lamb of God, I come.
>
> Just as I am, poor, wretched, blind,—
> Sight, riches, healing of the mind,
> Yea, all I need, in Thee to find,
>   O Lamb of God, I come.

XXVII

OUR LORD'S NEW COMMANDMENT: WHAT IS REQUIRED IN IT AND WHAT IS FORBIDDEN IN IT

So after He had washed their feet, and taken His garments, and was set down again, among other things He said to them, A new commandment I give unto you, that ye love one another; as I have loved you, that ye love one another. By this shall all men know that ye are My disciples, if ye have love to one another. Now, we are indebted to the Apostle Paul for the best exposition and application we possess of these new-covenant words of our Lord. And we shall closely follow the Apostle's exposition and application of our Lord's Communion Table words this Communion Table evening.

Well, then, according to Paul, the first outcome and evidence of a true communicant's love is this—that he "suffers long, and is kind." God is love, And one of the first and foremost of His attributes is His longsuffering. "The Lord God longsuffering" was one of the first revelations of Himself that God gave to Moses on the Mount. And from that memor able morning, all down the Old Testament, this gracious attribute of the divine nature was continually proclaimed by the great prophets. Till in the New Testament their longsuffering with all men becomes one of the surest marks of the true disciples of Christ. Now, all those who have been at the Lord's Table this day have had an assurance of God's longsuffering again sealed down to them; and they have engaged again that as Christ's disciples they will continue to show longsuffering toward all men, even as God has showed such longsuffering toward them. Ye call Me Master and Lord; and so I am. If I therefore have been so longsuffering toward you, so are you to be toward one another. Longsuffering, and all the time kind. And that, like Christ Himself, longsuffering to the end, and to the very end kind, like Christ upon the Cross. Now, my fellow-communicants, this is the point this evening with you and me. Have we any one in our eye from whom we have long and greatly suffered? And has God set that injurious man much before us at this communion season? When we were examining into ourselves before the Supper did some man rise up before us who causes us no little longsuffering? Well, then, let us keep our eye on that man, for he is supplied to us by God for our sanctification in our longsuffering toward him. What then is his name? And in what thing do you so suffer at his hands? Well, then, from this communion season let no bitterness, nor wrath, nor anger toward that man be found in you. Put away all these things, with all malice. And be kind to that man as often as God gives you opportunity. Always, and always, and always forgiving him, even as God, for Christ's sake, is always forgiving you.

And, then, "love envieth not." Now, what is it that is so definitely forbidden in the Tenth Commandment, and almost more so in our Lord's new Commandment? The Tenth Commandment forbiddeth all envying and all grieving at the good of our neighbour, and all evil affection toward anything that is his. And no wonder that envy is so divinely forbidden. For what a diabolical and inhuman state of mind is envy? Says Jonathan Edwards on the text: "He that is influenced by true Christian principle, though he may still find envy in his heart, he yet absolutely abhors himself on account of it. He sees and feels envy to be a most odious and most hateful state of mind and heart. And, therefore, he is terrified to find it in himself; he fights continually against it, and he cries to God continually to save him out of that horrible pit which still spews up its poison in his own heart." And then that great saint and great preacher turns to all true communicants, and says to them: "Do you ever find that wicked spirit moving within you? Do you ever detect yourselves grudging in your heart at any prosperous man? And does that devilish spirit continually lead you to think evil and to speak evil against that man? Then go to God at the moment and on the spot, and say to Him: Against Thee in this as well as against my brother have I sinned. I acknowledge this my great and wicked transgression, and this my so besetting sin is ever before me." Yes, what a never-to-be-told torture to a true communicant is the wicked indwelling of envy in his half-regenerate heart! Indeed, there is no greater torture in this life to a spiritually minded man. Says even the heathen Horace about it: "The Sicilian tyrants never invented a worse torture than that of envy." At the same time I congratulate you, my fellow-communicants, according as you keenly feel that terrible torture, for that terrible torture is the exact measure of the presence and the power of divine love in your hearts. And for you the day is at the door when you will be summoned to sit down at the Table above, where there will be nothing left anywhere in your hearts but love to God, and to all your glorified neighbours. No, love envieth not.

And love "vaunteth not itself." That is to say, love never boasts. It never brags. It never talks about itself. It lets other people talk about it, and when they speak its praises it shrinks into a corner. Love praises other men, and that with great eloquence; but it is absolutely silent about itself. Nebuchadnezzar had never been at the Lord's Table else he would never have vaunted himself, and said: "Is this not great Babylon that I have built by the might of my power, and for the honour of my majesty?" Nor would he have been driven forth from among men and made to dwell with the beasts of the field and made to eat grass like an ox. Nor had Herod ever had his feet washed by Christ else he would not have been eaten up of worms.

We hear continually about the wedding garment at our communion seasons. But there is no wedding garment more comely in the eyes of the King when He comes in to see the guests than that He sees us clothed from head to foot with humility. Be ye therefore found clothed with that beautiful garment at the Lord's Table, and at every table, till you are summoned up from the foot of the heavenly Table to sit beside the King Himself at the head of it. For God resisteth the proud, but giveth grace and glory to the humble.

"Is not puffed up." God help us! What are we, any of us, that we should be puffed up? We have nothing better, any of us, than our knowledge. And yet the Apostle tells us that knowledge, if it is without love, always puffs us up. But love, he says, even with little knowledge, always edifies us. Knowledge, says Paul, in his so plain-spoken way, makes a man a windbag. But love builds a man up, he says, like a living temple. "Our knowledge," says Bishop Sanderson, "at its very best is but a sorry thing, God knoweth. For he that hath most knowledge, yet what he knoweth is but a thousandth part of what he knoweth not." And Isaac Newton, Sanderson's contemporary, whose knowledge, in some things, came close upon God's own knowledge—Isaac Newton said a thing that was far better and far more edifying than all his amazing astronomical knowledge: "After all," he said, "I am but a child collecting shells on the seashore of knowledge." No; where true love is, and where there is enough of it, no man is ever puffed up with his knowledge, nor with anything else.

"Love doth not behave itself unseemly." That is to say, love doth nothing unbecoming, nothing unfitting, nothing inappropriate, nothing inopportune, nothing out of place. It doth nothing uncomely, nothing ungraceful, nothing ungainly, nothing rough nor rude, nothing vulgar, nothing ill-bred, nothing boorish, nothing in bad taste, nothing clownish, nothing uncouth, nothing unkempt. Love makes every man in whom it dwells a gentleman, and every woman in whom it dwells a lady. Paul's evangelical word seemliness is a fine word, and it describes a fine thing. For it is full of all decorum, and all fitness, and all true beauty of behaviour and of demeanour. Follow after love, then, and bring up your children to love God and their neighbour.

Love "seeketh not her own, is not easily provoked, thinketh no evil." She thinketh no evil of other disciples of Christ, even if they do not observe the ordinance of the Supper exactly as she observes it. Love does not think any real evil of them even if they kneel at the Supper when she sits at it, or sit at the Supper when she kneels at it. She thinketh no great evil of them even if they celebrate in Latin or in Greek when she celebrates in English. She doth not cast other communicants out of her synagogue because they have not had the happiness to be born and brought up in a home like hers, nor attended a minister's class like hers, nor subscribed an evangelical catechism or a confession of faith like hers. She thinketh as little evil as possible about them even though she cannot shut her eyes to the many evils that have descended and accumulated upon them. But all the time, as her own communions go on, she thinks better and better of all her fellow-communicants in all lands and in all churches, and worse and worse of herself. Love thinketh no evil neither in church matters, nor in national matters, nor in civic matters, nor in family matters, nor in any other matter whatsoever.

"Rejoiceth not in iniquity, but rejoiceth in the truth." That is to say, you do not take away any of her joy by telling her good news about anybody, even about her enemies. Nor do you add to her joy by telling her evil news about anybody, even about her enemies. She rejoices in the truth, even when the truth is to the advantage of those who do not love her. Love has none of our poisonous party spirit in her heart; she is of no sect, and she takes no side. Love always lives in the liberty, and in the universality, and in the impartiality of heaven. For now we know in part and now we prophesy in part. But when that which is perfect is come, then that which is in part shall be done away.

"Beareth all things, believeth all things, hopeth all things." Bear and forbear, says Epictetus, for that is the sum of human virtue between man and man. And believe all things, even almost an impostor's story, says Bishop Butler; and you know what an authority he is in all matters of Christian morals. Well, then, this is what Butler says on this matter of believing all things, in his golden sermon on love to our neighbour. " Though such is this world in which we live," says the Bishop, " that our growing experience of it must beget in us doubtfulness sometimes of the character of some men we meet, yet that doubtfulness ought not to be carried further than the nature of things makes necessary. And it is still true, even in the present state of things, bad as it is, that a real good man had rather be deceived than be suspicious ; had rather forego all his suspicions than run the risk of doing a hard thing and an unloving thing." And William Law impersonates and dramatises that principle of believing all things and hoping all things in his own unique way in his " Miranda and Her Two Hundred a Year." Let every enterprising communicant, every intellectually and morally enterprising communicant, and every one who can relish a delightful English style, read and lay to heart that masterpiece portrait of Miranda as it will be found in the entrancing gallery of " The Serious Call."

But all those who are at all following me in all that will be sure to say, Who is sufficient for all these things ? And they will ask how they are ever to attain to a love so pure and so rich and so many-sided as that. And how are they, the most self-loving and self-seeking of all men, ever to love like Christ, either in this world or in the world to come ? In two ways, my brethren, you will come to that. And, first, from this communion season begin as never before to practise all the thoughts, and all the words, and all the deeds of love. Practise makes perfection. Suffer every day then if need be, and all the time be kind to those who cause you suffering. And then even those who cause you your suffering will be compelled to confess whose disciples you are. Also, envy no man the possession of what God has given him to possess. Only pray for him that his possessions may be made a true blessing to him and his. Also, never open your mouth about yourself, lest all men say that you can by no possibility be a disciple of Christ, and lest they call you what they will be sure to call you as soon as they get rid of you. Again, when party spirit threatens to get entire dominion over you, always when you feel yourself getting unhappy and angry at the truth and the goodness on the other side, or elated with lies and wrongdoing on your side, that moment spit out that evil spirit, and never drink it in again as long as you live. Don't you know that the very devil is in it? And don't you know that if it is allowed it will make a devil of you? Neither read, therefore, nor hear, nor speak what degrades and corrupts a communicant into a slander-loving sinner. Keep out of your house every printed sheet that on either side poisons the wells of truth and love. And bear and forbear, both at home and abroad, lest Epictetus rise up against you at the last day. And judge not. Says James, Who art thou that judgest another? And when you must judge, let it be like Albert Bengel—*non sine scientia, non sine necessitate, non sine amore*—not without knowledge, not without necessity, and not without love. Practice will do it, and prayer; and especially prayer. And therefore let us offer now, and then let us take home with us, Bishop Butler's prayer at the end of his splendid sermon on love to our neighbour.

"O Almighty God," Butler prays, "inspire us with this divine principle of love. Kill in us all the seeds of envy and ill-will. And help us, by our cultivating within ourselves the love of our neighbour, to improve ourselves in the love of Thee. Thou hast placed us in various kindreds, in various friendships, in various relationships, as so many schools of discipline for our affections. Help us then, by the due exercise of our affections, to go on and to improve ourselves to perfection, till all partial and selfish affection shall be lost in that entire universal affection, and till Thou, O God, shalt be all, and in all. Amen."

XXVIII

WHO BELITTLES THE DISEASE BELITTLES THE DOCTOR

AFTER his seventh chapter to the Romans, which is the saddest chapter in all the Bible, Paul pens his eighth chapter, in which he is not an Apostle only but a prophet and a poet and a philosopher as well, and all of the first order. In this magnificent chapter Paul takes us back to the beginning of things, and then he takes us on to the end of things, and then he takes us down to the roots of things. There is a sweep of prophetic vision here that embraces all created things, with all their vicissitudes, from the day when God made man in His own image, down to that long-looked-for day when all things shall be made new, never again to become old. Revelation and inspiration, the truth of God and the thought of man, are all at their very highest here. And then the spiritual eloquence and the superb style of the Apostle all unite together to make the eighth of the Romans the loftiest, as well as the most consoling, chapter in all the Apostle's lofty and consoling Epistles.

Volumes, I may say, almost without number, have been written on the meaning of one single word in this great passage. From the earliest days, down to our own day, a discussion has been carried on among Pauline scholars concerning the meaning of the word *creature*, as that word occurs in the nineteenth verse. The question is, what exactly is the creature that has been made subject to vanity, not willingly? What is that whole creation which has been groaning and travailing in pain together until now? What is the creature itself, also, which shall be delivered from the bondage of corruption into the glorious liberty of the children of God? " For, the earnest expectation of the creature waiteth for the manifestation of the sons of God." Well, the ablest expounders of Paul have all come to this conclusion, that the Apostle has in his mind in this great passage, not any one part of creation, but this whole world of things, animate and inanimate, which Almighty God made at first for man, and made subject to man. And by the Holy Ghost, Paul here prophesies that this whole world of ours, which has so suffered from our sin, shall all share, correspondingly, in our redemption, and restitution, and glorification.

The readers of "Paradise Lost" can never forget John Milton's immortal rendering of the text. The groaning, and the travailing, and the pain of all created things, that came upon them all with the sin of Adam and Eve, is set before us with the most terrible power in that great poem.

> Earth trembled from her entrails, as again
> In pangs : and Nature gave a second groan :
> Sky lowered : and, muttering thunder, some sad drops
> Wept at completing of the mortal sin
>   Original . . . Nature first gave signs impressed
> On bird, beast, air : air suddenly eclipsed,
> After short blush of morn : nigh in their sight
> The bird of Jove stooped from his aery tour,
> Two birds of gayest plume before him drove :
> Down from the hill, the beast that reigns in woods,
> First hunter then, pursued a gentle brace,
> Goodliest of all the forest, hart and hind.

"And, not only they, but ourselves also, even we ourselves, groan within ourselves, waiting for the adoption, to wit, the redemption of our body." As Michael made fallen Adam to foresee :—

> "Immediately a place
> Before his eyes appeared, sad, noisome, dark :
> A lazar-house it seemed : wherein were laid
> Numbers of all diseased : all maladies
> Of ghastly spasms, or racking torture, qualms
> Of heart-sick agony, all feverous kinds,
> Convulsions, epilepsies, fierce catarrhs,
> Intestine stone, and ulcer, colic pangs,
> Demoniac phrenzy, moping melancholy,
> And moon-struck madness, pining atrophy,
> Marasmus, and wide-wasting pestilence,
> Dropsies, and asthmas, and joint-racking rheums.
> Dire was the tossing, deep the groans."
> "I yield it just," said Adam, "and submit."

I know. I know quite well. And I do not forget. Moses and Milton lived and wrote long before the days of Darwin and Herbert Spencer. For myself, I have read repeatedly and attentively all these four authors on the subject of this chapter. And I find plenty of room for all four in my Gospel doctrine, and in my Gospel hope. The "First Principles" was a great book with me in my student days. And that truly great book opened my eyes on outward nature in very many ways. But, with all that, I return continually to Moses, and to Paul, and to Milton. Receiving evolution, and development, and the origin of species, and the survival of the fittest, so far as I am able to understand these deep and difficult things; at the same time, the cosmology, the anthropology, the Christology, and the spiritual experience of the seventh and the eighth of the Romans are alone able to relieve my conscience, and to console my heart, and to satisfy my understanding, and to give scope to my imagination, and to anchor my hope. And, while reading eagerly all that is written, from day to day, about the amazing discoveries of our scientific men, I will return continually to Moses, and to Isaiah, and to Paul, and to John, till Paradise is restored.

What Paul means by the creature is a question of sacred scholarship. But what he means by the bondage of corruption is a question of religion, and of morals, and of personal experience. To study Paul on the creature we require to have a great apparatus of learned books. But to study him on the bondage of corruption we need nothing but our own sinful and unsanctified hearts. What then is this corruption, of which the Apostle here says such distressing things? Well, as we all know, to begin with, there is the corruption of a dead body. But the real corruption, the corruption of the text, is the corruption of a dead soul. There is the corruption of the grave. It was of that corruption that Martha spoke when she told our Lord to stand well back from her brother's grave because he had been dead four days. But, both our Lord and His Apostle warn us, with far more reason, and with far more urgency, to stand well back from the corruption of our own hearts, and of our neighbours' hearts, because we have been all our days and are still so dead in trespasses and in sins.

But it is not so much the corruption of our unsanctified hearts in itself only that the Apostle is here engaged upon. It is rather the bondage of that corruption. It is that dreadful bondage under which he himself, and all the still unsanctified children of God, continually labour. Paul has already given a whole chapter of this Epistle to that bondage as it still binds, and holds, and enslaves, and tortures himself. In terrible words that will last among us as long as God has a true saint under a great sanctification in this world, Paul is very bold to tell us about his own indescribable bondage to corruption. You all know his heartbroken cry. I would to God you all understood that holy and heartbroken cry of his, and every day made it your own! And, that it may be so—that I may, somewhat, help you to that—I will now make bold to give you a few examples of that indescribable bondage—as it is being experienced continually in the sin-corrupted hearts of all the Paul-like men and women among ourselves. And, as I give some examples of that bondage, you will all assent, or deny, for yourselves.

But where, and with what, shall I venture to

begin? Well, with this: since I must make a beginning with something, let it be with this. I was reading in Tacitus the other day and I came on this passage in that most pungent and most heart-searching of all the Roman writers. "We are all predisposed and inclined," he says, "to listen to those men who go about speaking ill of other people. We may know that the tale-bearer is a liar; but there is something in ourselves that makes us listen to him, and that makes us wish him to go on with his slanders against the men we do not love." But that deep observer of our corrupt hearts does not see at all so deep as Paul sees. Paul sees in himself, and in all his Roman converts, all that Tacitus here charges them with. But, if Paul had had the opportunity, he would have told Tacitus that the Christ, whose bare name only he had heard, had renewed and had changed the hearts of all who share His name. "We Christians," Paul would have said, "have still enough of Adam in our hearts to love to hear slanders and lies about certain men; but the moment after our Christian consciences rise up against our corrupt hearts, and we hate ourselves for ever listening to such false reports." I do not read in all Tacitus, bitter as he is against himself, what I read in Paul: "Oh! wretched man that I am! because I rejoice so naturally, sometimes, in hearing iniquity!"

Then, again, take Æsop for another corruption. You all remember his dog in the manger. The wretched cur did not wish to eat the littered straw himself: indeed, he could not eat it. But such was his doggish nature that he hated to see the hungry ox eating and enjoying the sweet straw. And we do not wish that post, or that possession, or that success, or that honour ourselves. We could neither use it, nor could we in any way enjoy it ourselves. But we are such hounds at heart, that we will hate to see another promoted to that post, to that possession, to that success, to that honour. Oh! miserable men that we are! We feel this abominable bondage bitterly; but we cannot, of ourselves, wholly cast it off. We can only cry to God against it; as Paul cried in grace, and has now been heard and delivered in glory.

Again, you will have some evil thing in your heart that burns to be spoken. But you know that it would be a great sin in you to speak it. And, knowing that, you put a bridle on your mouth, through a thousand temptations to speak. But, suddenly, some evil day, the corruption in your heart becomes too strong for your bridle, and out the evil word comes! And then it is no sooner out than you could bite out your sinful tongue, such is your remorse and your misery. And your heart is broken for days after; and you are back at the blood of Christ, for days and weeks after, as much as if you had committed some great crime that had scandalised the whole community. So bitterly do you feel your bondage to the deep corruption that still lurks in your unsanctified heart.

Again, some man's name will come up incidentally in a conversation; or your eye will light on his name accidentally, say in a newspaper; and that moment, like gunpowder, your heart will be on fire against that man, who is, all the time, so innocent, and so unsuspecting of your ill-will. Not that you would hurt a hair of his head, even if it were in your power to do so. Divine grace would hold your hands from hurting him, but even divine grace has not yet healed your heart from hating him. "That which I do," sobbed Paul, falling on his face, "I allow not; for, what I would, that do I not; but what I hate, that do I."

Then again take this same bondage to corruption in another sphere of our daily life. You are a preacher, or you are some kind of public speaker, or public performer of some kind or other. Now, do what you will: watch, and pray, and crucify yourself, as you will; I defy you not to be sinfully puffed up with success and with praise; and then as sinfully cast down, and your peace of mind poisoned with faultfinding, and with correction, and with blame, and with neglect. You profess that you love your art and your office above everything. But there are times when you are compelled to confess that you love your pitiful self more than all the arts and all the offices in the world. Perish preaching, and speaking, and singing, and playing, and everything else, if I do not get the applause and the praise that my hungry heart alone lives upon! "In my preaching," says Bunyan, "I have often been tempted to pride and to lifting up of heart. And, though I dare not say that I have not been infected with this, yet, truly, the Lord, of His great mercy, hath so carried it toward me, that, for the most part, I have had but small joy to give way to such a thing. For, it hath been my everyday's portion to be let into the evil of my own heart, and still made to see such a multitude of corruptions and infirmities in my heart, that it hath caused hangings down of my head under all my gifts and attainments. I have felt this thorn in my flesh to be the very God of Mercy to me."

And springing out of that, there is, perhaps, no corruption so universal, and no bondage so bitter, to some men, as that diabolical bondage to which these utterances were given on that hillside which cleanses him who climbs.

> Though Sapia named,
> In sapience I excelled not: gladder far
> Of others' hurt than of the good befel myself.

And, again :

> Guido of Duca know thee that I am.
> Envy so parched my blood, that had I seen
> A fellow-man made joyous, thou hadst marked
> A livid paleness overspread my cheek.
> Such harvest reap I of the seed I sowed.

It is not lack of matter, but lack of time, that makes me stop my examples and illustrations of our remaining corruption of heart and life. But out of all that, I must share one or two lessons with you before I close. And first:

1. It is only the learned who feel that they are ignorant. And it is only the largely sanctified who feel that they are still so sinful. And it is only the growingly and almost perfectly holy who feel that

they are still held fast in the bondage of corruption. Some time after Duncan Matheson's remarkable conversion, he came across the original of David Elginbrod one day in the square of Huntly. "How are you getting on, Duncan?" asked the old saint. "Don't speak to me," said Duncan, hanging his head; "I am a mass of corruption. I never was truly converted at all." "No fear, Duncan," said the experienced saint, "the dead feel no corruption. They never cry Unclean! unclean! in the grave." No; Paul never cried to God that he was sold under sin, so long as he was taking the first prizes in Gamaliel's school.

2. The second lesson is this: No bondage, no liberty; little bondage, little liberty; a great bondage, a great liberty. "He who makes little of his disease," says Goodwin, "makes little of his doctor."

3. And the third lesson is this: As regards Scriptures like this, and sermons like this, the same master in Israel says: "Here it may be truly said, that of all discourses they are by far the most difficult that are made concerning the inward workings of sin and grace. As no study is more hard than anatomy, which discourseth of the parts of the human body; unless a man hath seen a human body anatomised: and then, nothing is more easy, certain, and evident. So also is it in an anatomy-lecture of the mind and the heart."

4. And this is the fourth lesson: If Paul's anatomical chapters have come home to your heart and conscience, then this will be one of your favourite

questions and answers in your Shorter Catechism: "The souls of believers are at their death made perfect in holiness, and do immediately pass into the glorious liberty of the children of God." And this will be one of your favourite psalms both in grace and in glory :—

> When Zion's bondage God turned back,
>   As men that dream'd were we.
> Then filled with laughter was our mouth,
>   Our tongue with melody.
>
> That man who, bearing precious seed,
>   In going forth doth mourn,
> He, doubtless, bringing back his sheaves,
>   Rejoicing shall return.